LEARNING 100

LANGUAGE CLUES
Vocabulary
Spelling
Prediction

Study Guide
DA
Second Edition

Author
Alan Petraske

Spelling Author and Prediction Consultant
Helen Frackenpohl Morris

Consultant
H. Alan Robinson

Professor of Reading
Hofstra University
Hempstead, New York

ISBN 1-56260-689-1

2 3 4 5 6 7 8 9 10 PO 00 99 98 97 96

To the Student

Welcome to the Language Clues program. Through this program, you will:

- Learn the meaning and use of 400 important words
- Learn to spell these 400 words correctly
- Become skilled in predicting the ideas you meet in reading

The program has three parts:

- Vocabulary
- Spelling
- Prediction

At the beginning of each part, you will find instructions on how to use that part. Use the Contents below to find the introduction to each part.

Contents

Why is it important to have a large vocabulary? Knowing the meanings of a large number of words will help you in listening and reading, as well as in speaking and writing.

First let's talk about listening and reading. If you know the meanings of most of the words used by a speaker or writer, you have a much better chance of understanding what that person is saying. The more words you know, the more easily you can understand.

The same thing applies to speaking and writing. If you have a large vocabulary, you can express your ideas more clearly. You can get across exactly what you mean instead of saying "you know," or "you know what I mean."

A good way to improve your vocabulary is to watch for new words whenever you read. But what do you do when you come across a word you don't know? Do you stop to look it up in a dictionary? Do you sound it out? Or do you look at the way the word is used in a sentence?

There are many ways to learn the meaning of a strange word. But the quickest and often the easiest way is knowing how to use the **context**. This means using the other words in a sentence or paragraph to figure out the meaning of the new word. When you use the context, you use the meaning of all the other words to unlock the meaning of the word you do not know.

Sometimes the context will not tell you all you want to know about a word. Then you will want to look it up in a dictionary. The dictionary will tell you how to pronounce the word and will give you one or more meanings for the word. If there is more than one meaning, you can use the context to find the meaning you want.

The twenty Vocabulary lessons in this section of Language Clues will help you learn:

- How to use context clues to find word meanings
- How to use a dictionary to find word meanings
- 400 words and their meanings

There are three parts in each vocabulary lesson:

- Words in Sentences
- Word Play
- Words in Stories

After every five lessons, there is a Review lesson where you can find out how well you remember the 100 words you learned.

How to Do "Cloze" Exercises

Many of the exercises in the Vocabulary lessons are "cloze" exercises. This means that you have to choose a word to fill in the blank in a sentence. Here are some tips on how to do cloze exercises. Study this section carefully. Then refer back to these tips whenever you need to do so.

Experience Clues

Your experience will help you fill many of the blanks in the sentences. Suppose you see "roast _____ sandwich" and the three choices are **paint**, **desk**, and **beef**. Your experience tells you that **beef** is the right answer. Your experience will help you figure out the meanings of many words.

You also know a great deal about different kinds of words and how they should be used in sentences. Each sentence contains many clues to the kind of word that belongs in the blank.

Noun Clues

A *noun* is a word that names a person, place, or thing. A *noun marker* is a word that tells you a noun will follow. Here are some noun markers:

a an some that the this

one, two, three (and other number words)

When you see any one of these noun markers in front of a blank, chances are good that a noun will follow, as in these examples:

this party   **two** motorcycles   **a** job

Which words belong in these blanks?
The _____ is green. (tree, skip)
Some _____ are kind. (sitting, people)

Another kind of noun clue is the *possessive*. The clue to a possessive is the ending **'s** or words like **my**, **her**, **his**, **their**, **your**, **our**, and **its**. Here are some possessives:

her book   **Bill's** job   **our** family

Possessives are usually followed by nouns.

Which words belong in these blanks?
Ramon's _____ is sharp. (pencil, huge)
Gretchen's _____ is interesting. (story, writes)
My _____ are going with me. (brothers, green)

Verb Clues

Every complete sentence has a *verb*, which tells you about an action or the way something is or was.

The dog **bit** the child.
The house **is** warm today.

Which words belong in these blanks?

John _____ the sandwich. (ate, pretty)

Elaine _____ a careful worker. (desk, is)

Helping words tell you a verb will follow. Some helping words are:

> can could has have will would
>
> has been   have been

Here are some sentences with helping words.

> We **have been** waiting a long time.
>
> John **can** run faster than Peter.

Which words belong in these blanks?

> The dog will _____ home soon. (blue, come)
>
> She would _____ a car for her birthday. (like, tree)

Adjective Clues

If there is a blank between a noun marker and a noun, you will probably need to fill it with an *adjective*. An adjective tells something about a noun.

> a **cozy** room   a **delicious** salad

Choose a word that belongs in each blank.

> The _____ wind made me shiver. (start, cold)
>
> I love my _____ coat. (new, stand)

Adverb Clues

If there is a blank before or after a verb or in between a helping verb and a verb, you can probably fill it with an *adverb*. Adverbs tell how or how often an action took place. Adverbs can also tell why, where, or when an action took place. Adverbs often end with *ly*, as in these examples:

> Jack ran **swiftly** to the mailbox.
>
> When the phone rings, I answer **quickly**.

Choose a word to fit in each blank.

> We _____ walk to school. (usually, picture)
>
> The little girl sat _____ . (quietly, book)

Knowing how words work gives you many clues that will help you choose the best word to fill each blank.

How to Use the Mini-Dictionary

In each lesson, you will find a Mini-Dictionary. It contains entries for all of the words in the lesson. The words are arranged in alphabetical order.

First find the entry for a word you want. Then make sure you know how to pronounce the word.

Look at the pronunciation key on the inside back cover if you need help with any of the sounds in the word.

Next you need to find the meaning of the word. Use the clues in the sentence to decide what kind of meaning you are looking for. Read through the definitions until you find the correct meaning for the word as it is used in the blank in the sentence.

Try this example. The sentence says, "Someone sent up a _____ in order to get help."

You have a choice of "accident" or "flare." You know that "accident" doesn't make sense in this blank. Suppose you aren't sure what "flare" means.

Here is the Mini-Dictionary entry for flare:

flare (fler *or* flar), **1** flame up briefly or unsteadily, sometimes with smoke: *A gust of wind made the torches flare.* **2** blaze; bright, brief, unsteady flame: *The flare of a match showed us his face.* **3** a dazzling light that burns for a short time, used for signaling or lighting up a battlefield: *The Coast Guard vessel responded to the flare sent up from the lifeboat.* **4** a sudden outburst: *a flare of anger.* **5** spread out in the shape of a bell: *These pants flare at the bottom.* **6** spreading out into a bell shape: *the flare of a skirt.* 1,5 *verb,* **flared, flar ing;** 2-4,6 *noun.*
flare up, burst into sudden anger or violence.

First you have to decide what kind of word you are looking for. The noun marker "a" in the sentence tells you that the missing word is a noun.

Look at the first definition. This definition doesn't fit because it's for a verb, not for the name of something. The second definition is close, but the sentence that follows tells you that this kind of flare doesn't last very long—not long enough to get help at the scene of an accident.

Read the third definition and the sentence that follows it. The third definition works in the sentence. "A dazzling light that burns for a short time" would definitely attract the attention of anyone who might be able to help.

Whenever you use the Mini-Dictionary, make sure to choose the definition that fits the sentence in the exercise.

How to Complete the Vocabulary Lessons

Write all answers on an answer sheet, not in the book. Your teacher will tell you what to write at the top of your answer sheet. With each exercise, you will be given directions for setting up your answer sheet.

Check your answers with the Answer Key that begins on page 114. If you get an answer wrong, look back to see why you are wrong. If you can't figure out why you are wrong, check with your teacher.

ac ci dent (ak′sə dənt), **1** something harmful or unlucky that happens: *She was hurt in an automobile accident.* **2** something that happens without being planned, intended, wanted, or known in advance: *A series of lucky accidents led the explorer to his discovery. noun.*

ac tu al ly (ak′chü ə lē), really; in fact: *Are you actually going to camp this summer or just wishing to go? adverb.*

an ces tor (an′ses′tər), person from whom one is directly descended. Your grandfathers, your grandmothers, and so on back, are your ancestors. *noun.*

bat ter y (bat′ər ē), **1** a single electric cell: *Most flashlights work on two batteries.* **2** set of two or more electric cells that produce electric current. Batteries provide the current that starts automobile and truck engines. **3** any set of similar or connected things: *The mayor spoke before a battery of television cameras.* **4** set of big guns for combined action in attack or defense: *Four batteries began firing.* **5** (in baseball) the pitcher and catcher together. *noun, plural* **bat ter ies.**

beef (bēf), **1** meat from a steer, cow, or bull. **2** steer, cow, or bull when full-grown and fattened for food. *noun.*

cel e brate (sel′ə brāt), **1** observe (a special time or day) with the proper activities: *We celebrated my birthday with a party and cake and ice cream.* **2** perform publicly with the proper ceremonies and rites: *The priest celebrates Mass in church.* **3** have a gay time: *When the children saw the snow, they celebrated. verb,* **cel e brat ed, cel e brat ing.**

com mand (kə mand′), **1** give an order to; order; direct. **2** order; direction. **3** be in authority over; have power over; be master of. **4** possession of authority; power; control. **5** the soldiers or ships or a region under a person who has the right to command them. **6** control by position; rise high above; overlook. **7** be able to have and use. **8** ability to have and use. "She has an excellent command of English" means that she speaks it unusually well. **9** deserve and get. 1,3,6,7,9 *verb,* 2,4,5,8 *noun.* (*Definition adapted*)

con ven ient (kən vē′nyənt), **1** suitable; saving trouble; well arranged; easy to use: *take a convenient bus, live in a convenient house.* **2** easily done; not troublesome: *Will it be convenient for you to bring your lunch to school?* **3** within easy reach; handy: *meet at a convenient place. adjective.*

cur i os i ty (kyùr′ē os′ə tē), **1** eager desire to know: *Curiosity got the better of me, and I opened the unmarked box.* **2** a strange, rare object: *One of his curiosities was a cane made of the horn of a deer. noun, plural* **cur i os i ties.**

dis cov er y (dis kuv′ər ē), **1** finding out; seeing or learning of something for the first time: *Balboa's discovery of the Pacific Ocean occurred in 1513.* **2** thing found out: *One of Benjamin Franklin's discoveries was that lightning is electricity. noun, plural* **dis cov er ies.**

en e my (en′ə mē), **1** person or group that hates or tries to harm another. Two countries fighting against each other are enemies. **2** anything that will harm: *Frost is an enemy of flowers. noun, plural* **en e mies.**

en ve lope (en′və lōp), **1** a paper cover in which a letter or anything flat can be mailed. It can usually be folded over and sealed by wetting a gummed edge. **2** wrapper; covering. *noun.*

fact (fakt), **1** thing known to be true; thing known to have happened: *It is a fact that the Pilgrims sailed to America on the Mayflower in 1620.* **2** what is true; truth: *The fact is, I did not want to go to the dance.* **3** thing said or supposed to be true or to have really happened: *We doubted his facts. noun.*

fa mil iar (fə mil′yər), **1** well-known; common: *a familiar face. A knife is a familiar tool. French was as familiar to him as English.* **2** well acquainted: *She is familiar with French and English.* **3** close; personal; intimate: *Those familiar friends know each other very well.* **4** too friendly; forward: *His manner is too familiar. adjective.*

flare (fler *or* flar), **1** flame up briefly or unsteadily, sometimes with smoke: *A gust of wind made the torches flare.* **2** blaze; bright, brief, unsteady flame: *The flare of a match showed us his face.* **3** a dazzling light that burns for a short time, used for signaling or lighting up a battlefield: *The Coast Guard vessel responded to the flare sent up from the lifeboat.* **4** a sudden outburst: *a flare of anger.* **5** spread out in the shape of a bell: *These pants flare at the bottom.* **6** spreading out into a bell shape: *the flare of a skirt.* 1,5 *verb,* **flared, flar ing;** 2-4,6 *noun.*

fro zen (frō′zn), **1** hardened with cold; turned into ice: *a river frozen over, frozen sherbet.* **2** very cold: *My hands are frozen; I need some gloves.* **3** preserved by being subjected to low temperatures: *frozen foods.* **4** killed or injured by frost: *frozen flowers.* **5** covered or clogged with ice: *frozen water pipes.* **6** cold and unfeeling: *a frozen heart, a frozen stare.* **7** too frightened or stiff to move: *frozen to the spot in horror.* **8** See **freeze.** *The water has frozen to ice.* 1-7 *adjective,* 8 *verb.*

in for ma tion (in′fər mā′shən), **1** knowledge given or received of some fact or circumstance; news: *We have just received information of the astronauts' safe landing.* **2** things known; facts: *A dictionary contains much information about words.* **3** informing: *A guidebook is for the information of travelers. noun.*

in stant (in′stənt), **1** a particular moment: *Stop talking this instant!* **2** moment of time: *He paused for an instant.* **3** without delay; immediate: *The medicine gave instant relief from pain.* **4** prepared beforehand and requiring little or no cooking, mixing, or additional ingredients: *instant coffee, instant pudding.* 1,2 *noun,* 3,4 *adjective.*

pur pose (pėr′pəs), a plan; aim; intention; something one has in mind to get or do: *Her purpose in coming to see us was to ask for a donation to the hospital fund. noun.*
on purpose, with a purpose; not by accident: *He tripped me on purpose.*

re al ize (rē′ə līz), **1** understand clearly: *I realize how hard you worked.* **2** make real: *Her uncle's present made it possible for her to realize the dream of going to college. verb,* **re al ized, re al iz ing.**

Words in Sentences

Number from 1 to 20 on your answer sheet. Next to each numeral, write the word that belongs on that blank line in the sentence. Use the words at the left of each sentence. Use the Mini-Dictionary on the opposite page to find the meaning(s) of each word you don't know.

___ battery ___
___ realize ___
___ fact ___

Jack didn't ____1____ that the ____2____ in the car was dead until he was faced with the ____3____ that the car wouldn't start.

___ enemy ___
___ instant ___
___ command ___

The captain gave the ____4____ to attack the ____5____ he saw the ____6____ cross the bridge.

___ accident ___
___ flare ___

After the ____7____, someone sent up a ____8____ in order to get help.

___ celebrate ___
___ ancestor ___

My oldest living ____9____ will ____10____ her 96th birthday tomorrow.

___ frozen ___
___ beef ___
___ convenient ___

When you asked me over for a roast ____11____ dinner, I didn't know that you meant a TV dinner. I don't care if it is more ____12____. I like my meat fresh rather than ____13____.

___ purpose ___
___ information ___
___ familiar ___

What is the ____14____ of asking me that question again? I'm not ____15____ with that book, so I can't give you the ____16____ you want.

___ envelope ___
___ curiosity ___

It was ____17____ that made me open the ____18____ addressed to my wife.

___ actually ___
___ discovery ___

Christopher Columbus's ____19____ of America was ____20____ made possible by Spain's Queen Isabella.

—— **Check your answers with the key.** ——

5

Word Play

A

Number from 21 to 30 on your answer sheet. Next to each numeral, write the word from the box that completes the sentence. One has been done for you.

accident	enemy
ancestor	fact
celebrate	flare
command	information
curiosity	purpose
discovery	

B

Number from 31 to 40 on your answer sheet. Next to each numeral, write the word from the box that completes the group.

actually	instant
beef	envelope
convenient	flare
battery	realize
familiar	frozen

A

EXAMPLE: A burning match is an example of a light that will ___*flare*___ .

21. A country that is at war with yours is an example of an _____ .

22. Spilled milk is an example of an _____ .

23. Finding America was an example of a _____ .

24. Wondering what's inside a package is an example of _____ .

25. Having a large party is an example of a way to _____ .

26. A great-grandmother is an example of an _____ .

27. "Forward, march!" is an example of a _____ .

28. "The earth is round" is an example of a _____ .

29. "We plan to climb the mountain" is an example of a _____ .

30. "The sky is green" is an example of wrong _____ .

—— Check your answers with the key. ——

B

You may have seen word groups like those in the examples that follow:

EXAMPLE: dark : light : : left : _____

We say: **Dark** goes with **light** in the same way that **left** goes with _____ . **Dark** and **light** are *opposites*. The word that goes on the blank must be the *opposite* of **left**. **Right** is the *opposite* of **left**.

So: dark : light : : left : *right*

EXAMPLE: corn : vegetable : : apple : _____

We say: **Corn** goes with **vegetable** in the same way that **apple** goes with _____ . **Corn** is an *example* of a **vegetable**. **Apple** is an *example* of the word that goes on the line. **Apple** is an *example* of a **fruit**.

So: corn : vegetable : : apple : fruit

31. careful : careless : : melted : _____
32. autumn : fall : : moment : _____
33. meal : breakfast : : light : _____
34. strike : hit : : understand : _____
35. correct : right : : easy-to-use : _____
36. loud : soft : : strange : _____
37. month : April : : meat : _____
38. quickly : rapidly : : truly : _____
39. gift : package : : letter : _____
40. kite : wind : : flashlight : _____

—— Check your answers with the key. ——

Before you do the Words in Stories exercise, take the *Spelling Recognition Test* on page 128 and check your answers with the key at the back of the book.

Number from 41 to 45 on your answer sheet. Next to each numeral, write the word from the box that completes the sentence.

battery	flare
command	information
enemy	

Number from 46 to 50 on your answer sheet. Next to each numeral, write the word from the box that completes the sentence.

beef	instant
fact	purpose
frozen	

Number from 51 to 55 on your answer sheet. Next to each numeral, write the word from the box that completes the sentence.

accident	familiar
ancestor	realize
convenient	

Number from 56 to 60 on your answer sheet. Next to each numeral, write the word from the box that completes the sentence.

actually	discovery
celebrate	envelope
curiosity	

A

After the battle near the edge of a large forest, six of the captain's men were missing. After two days of searching, there was no further ____41____ about the missing men. No one had learned anything new about them. Perhaps their field radio wasn't working because it had a dead ____42____. Perhaps they had been trapped by the ____43____. The captain gave the order to keep searching for the lost men in his ____44____.

Each rescue team flew over a different part of the forest in a small plane. Finally one team saw the men's signal: the bright light of a ____45____ as it shot up into the sky. The missing men were alive.

B

Jack Flash decided to open a fast-food shop. His friends tried to change Jack's plans, but Jack stuck to his ____46____. He said all his food would be cooked and quickly ____47____ at a huge freezing plant before it was sent to his shop.

When someone ordered a roast ____48____ sandwich, Jack would just take the meat from his freezer. Jack said it took only an ____49____ to heat up, but really it took longer than that to get hot. He often said things that were not quite true. Jack never let himself be held back by a ____50____!

C

Carla's parents had died in an automobile ____51____. The following year, she decided to visit her great-aunt Rosa in Mexico City. Carla took a plane to Mexico City. It was the most ____52____ way of getting there from Ohio.

Great-aunt Rosa was much too old to show Carla around Mexico City, but she told many a good story. The one Carla liked best was about Pedro, a Spanish ____53____ of theirs. Great-aunt Rosa said that Pedro, a sailor, had come over to America from Spain, long before the Pilgrims landed at Plymouth Rock in Massachusetts.

At the end of the visit, just before Carla had to board her plane, great-aunt Rosa gave her a small package and said, "This has been in our family for hundreds of years. It is yours now."

Carla thanked great-aunt Rosa, but did not have a chance to open the package until her plane was in the air. Inside the package, Carla found a very small and very old painting of a young sailor who looked strangely ____54____. It took Carla only a moment to ____55____ that the painting must be of Pedro.

D

Bill and I didn't know what was in the fat ____56____ we found in the park. We thought there might be a very long letter inside, but of course we couldn't ____57____ know until we had opened it. Our ____58____ made us look inside. We saw $500 in new bills!

Our ____59____ made us so happy, we began to dance around. Bill wanted to throw a big party to ____60____ our good luck, but I told him we'd have to put off the party. First we had to check with the police to see if anyone had asked if the money had been found.

— **Check your answers with the key.** —

a gree (ə grē′), **1** have the same opinion: *We all agree in liking the teacher. I agree with your argument.* **2** be in harmony: *Your story agrees with mine.* **3** get along well together: *Brothers and sisters don't always agree as well as they should.* **4** say that one is willing; consent: *He agreed to go with us.* verb, **a greed, a gree ing.**

ar gue (är′gyü), **1** discuss with someone who disagrees: *He argued with his sister about who should wash the dishes.* **2** give reasons for or against something: *The children argued about who should wash the dishes.* **3** persuade by giving reasons: *They argued me into going.* verb, **ar gued, ar gu ing.**

busi ness (biz′nis), **1** thing that one is busy at; work; occupation: *A carpenter's business is building.* **2** matter; affair: *I am tired of the whole business.* **3** buying and selling; trade: *This hardware store does a big business in tools.* **4** a store, factory, or other commercial enterprise: *They sold the bakery business.* noun, plural **busi ness es** for 4.

death (deth), **1** dying; the ending of life in people, animals, or plants: *The old man's death was calm and peaceful.* **2** any ending that is like dying: *the death of an empire, the death of one's hopes.* **3** being dead: *In death his heart was still.* noun.

ex pert (ek′spėrt′ for 1; ek spėrt′ or ek′spėrt′ for 2), **1** person who has much skill or who knows a great deal about some special thing: *She is an expert at fishing.* **2** having much skill; knowing a great deal about some special thing: *an expert painter.* 1 noun, 2 adjective.

ex pla na tion (ek′splə nā′shən), **1** explaining; clearing up a difficulty or mistake: *He did not understand the teacher's explanation of multiplication.* **2** something that explains: *This diagram is a good explanation of how an automobile engine works.* noun.

gen er al (jen′ər əl), **1** of all; for all; from all: *A government takes care of the general welfare of its citizens.* **2** widespread; not limited to a few; for many; from many: *There is a general interest in television.* **3** not detailed: *The teacher gave us only general instructions.* **4** not special: *a general store, a general magazine. A general reader reads different kinds of books.* **5** chief: *The Attorney General is the head of the legal department of the government.* **6** a high officer in command of many soldiers in an army. 1-5 adjective, 6 noun.

in general, usually; commonly: *She is friendly with me in general, but she was particularly friendly today.*

gov ern ment (guv′ərn mənt), **1** the ruling of a country, state, district, or city: *local government.* **2** person or persons ruling a country, state, district, or city at any time: *The government of the United States consists of the President and the cabinet, the Congress, and the Supreme Court.* **3** system of ruling: *The United States has a democratic form of government.* **4** rule; control. noun.

hab it (hab′it), **1** custom; practice. Doing a thing over and over again makes it a habit. *Form the habit of brushing your teeth after every meal.* **2** the clothing worn by members of some religious orders. Monks and nuns often wear habits. noun.

hes i tate (hez′ə tāt), **1** hold back; feel doubtful; be undecided; show that one has not yet made up one's mind: *I hesitated about taking his side until I knew the whole story.* **2** feel that perhaps one shouldn't; not wish to: *I hesitated to ask you; you were so busy.* **3** stop for an instant; pause: *She hesitated before asking the question.* **4** speak with short stops or pauses; stammer. verb, **hes i tat ed, hes i tat ing.**

hob by (hob′ē), something a person likes to do as a pastime: *Our teacher's hobby is gardening.* noun, plural **hob bies.**

im pa tient (im pā′shənt), **1** not patient; not willing to bear delay, opposition, pain, or bother: *He is impatient with his little brother.* **2** uneasy and eager; restless: *The horses are impatient to start in the race.* **3** showing lack of patience: *an impatient answer.* adjective.

mar ried (mar′ēd), **1** living together as husband and wife: *a married couple.* **2** having a husband or wife: *a married man.* **3** of husband and wife: *Married life has many rewards.* adjective.

neph ew (nef′yü), son of one's brother or sister; son of one's brother-in-law or sister-in-law. noun.

op po site (op′ə zit), **1** placed against; as different in direction as can be; face to face; back to back: *The house straight across the street is opposite to ours.* **2** as different as can be; just contrary: *North and south are opposite directions. Sour is opposite to sweet.* **3** thing or person as different as can be: *Night is the opposite of day. A saint is the opposite of a sinner.* 1,2 adjective, 3 noun.

par tic u lar (pər tik′yə lər), **1** apart from others; considered separately; single: *That particular chair is already sold.* **2** belonging to some one person, thing, group, or occasion: *His particular task is to care for the dog.* **3** different from others; unusual; special: *This vacation was of particular importance to her, for she was going to Brazil. He is a particular friend of mine.* **4** hard to please; wanting everything to be just right; very careful: *They are very particular; nothing but the best will do.* **5** an individual part; item; point: *All the particulars of the accident are now known.* 1-4 adjective, 5 noun.

in particular, especially: *We strolled around, not going anywhere in particular.*

pa tient (pā′shənt), **1** having patience; showing patience: *The teacher was patient with the class.* **2** person who is being treated by a doctor. 1 adjective, 2 noun.

pos ses sion (pə zesh′ən), **1** possessing; holding: *I have in my possession the books you lost.* **2** ownership: *On her 21st birthday she came into possession of $50,000.* **3** thing possessed; property: *Please move your possessions from my room.* **4** territory under the rule of a country: *Guam is a possession of the United States.* **5** self-control. noun.

Tues day (tüz′dē or tyüz′dē), the third day of the week; the day after Monday. noun.

yes ter day (yes′tər dē), **1** the day before today: *Yesterday was cold and rainy.* **2** on the day before today: *It rained yesterday.* **3** the recent past: *We are often amused by the fashions of yesterday.* 1,3 noun, 2 adverb.

Words in Sentences

Number from 1 to 20 on your answer sheet. Next to each numeral, write the word that belongs on that blank line in the sentence. Use the words at the left of each sentence. Use the Mini-Dictionary on the opposite page to find the meaning(s) of each word you don't know.

__yesterday__

__patient__

The ____1____ now waiting in the doctor's office was supposed to have come in ____2____ .

__explanation__

__argue__

__opposite__

Whenever I say one thing, he says the ____3____ . That might be one ____4____ of why we ____5____ so much.

__death__

__general__

In the army, a ____6____ does not face ____7____ as often as the men in the front lines.

__government__

__particular__

People who work in ____8____ offices must be very ____9____ about keeping careful records.

__nephew__

__married__

__impatient__

She is ____10____ for her ____11____ to find the right woman and get ____12____ .

__business__

__expert__

__hesitate__

He would ____13____ to go into ____14____ with someone who is not already an ____15____ .

__habit__

__hobby__

__Tuesday__

Every day except ____16____ , Uncle Tony spends some time in the garden. We think gardening is a good ____17____ , but sometimes Uncle Tony's ____18____ of talking to the plants drives us crazy.

__possession__

__agree__

Do you ____19____ that a car is your most important ____20____ ?

—— **Check your answers with the key.** ——

9

A

Number from 21 to 25 on your answer sheet. Next to each numeral, write the word from the box that completes the sentence.

nephew	possession
patient	general
Tuesday	

B

Number from 26 to 30 on your answer sheet. Next to each numeral, write the word from the box that means about the **same** as the word(s) at the right.

business	habit
government	argue
opposite	

C

Number from 31 to 40 on your answer sheet. Next to each numeral, write the word from the box that means about the **opposite** of the word(s) at the right.

married	explanation
particular	expert
death	agree
hesitate	hobby
yesterday	impatient

A

21. That woman with five stars on her hat could be a _____ .
22. That man in the doctor's office could be a _____ .
23. That club could hold its next meeting on a _____ .
24. That boy could be someone's _____ .
25. That clock could be someone's _____ .

—— **Check your answers with the key.** ——

B

26. tools : repair : : reason : _____
27. paper : envelope : : cloth : _____
28. captain : ship : : president : _____
29. enemy : friend : : same : _____
30. bird : animal : : store : _____

—— **Check your answers with the key.** ——

C

31. general _____
32. question _____
33. beginner _____
34. patient _____
35. single _____
36. business _____
37. begin at once _____
38. life _____
39. argue _____
40. tomorrow _____

—— **Check your answers with the key.** ——

Before you do the Words in Stories exercise, take the *Spelling Recognition Test* on page 129 and check your answers with the key at the back of the book.

Number from 41 to 45 on your answer sheet. Next to each numeral, write the word from the box that completes the sentence.

hesitate	hobby
habit	death
agree	

Number from 46 to 50 on your answer sheet. Next to each numeral, write the word from the box that completes the sentence.

patient	particular
opposite	general
government	

C

Number from 51 to 55 on your answer sheet. Next to each numeral, write the word from the box that completes the sentence.

explanation	Tuesday
expert	argue
business	

Number from 56 to 60 on your answer sheet. Next to each numeral, write the word from the box that completes the sentence.

possession	yesterday
impatient	nephew
married	

A

When she turned sixty-five, Emma decided to stop working, but she wondered how she would spend each day away from the office. Working had become a _____ 41 _____ . Emma's friends told her that raising flowers would be a good _____ 42 _____ .

After working in the garden for a few months, Emma had to _____ 43 _____ , but she wanted to lead a more useful life. She knew her _____ 44 _____ would come soon enough.

When someone from Emma's church called and asked her if she could help out at the office, Emma said "yes" right away. She didn't _____ 45 _____ for a minute.

B

Jim spent most of his life in the mountains searching for a lost silver mine. The mountain lands were open to everyone because they were owned by the _____ 46 _____ .

Many people had looked for this mine on the south side of the mountains in a _____ 47 _____ sort of way. But Jim knew of one _____ 48 _____ place that was hard to get to because it was on the _____ 49 _____ side of the mountains, far from everything. Each spring Jim returned to search for the mine but failed to find it. He knew that sooner or later he would find the mine and strike it rich. Until then, Jim would remain a poor but _____ 50 _____ man.

C

Lee Brown had not shown up for work on _____ 51 _____ , but he came in early the next day. Shortly after he arrived, Holly Jayson, who owns the _____ 52 _____ , came up to him and said, "I want an _____ 53 _____ for why you did not show up for work the other day!"

Lee was very angry at being spoken to that way. He felt like telling Holly to go find herself somebody else who was as _____ 54 _____ as he at fixing cars—if she could! But he stopped himself. Holly paid well, and he needed this job. Lee decided it would be best not to _____ 55 _____ with Holly. Instead, Lee calmly said, "I wasn't here on Tuesday, because you had given me the day off."

From the surprised look on Holly's face, Lee knew she really had forgotten about that. But being Holly, all she said was, "Well, don't let it happen again!" Then she banged the door behind her as she left. Lee wondered if he would ever get used to working for Holly Jayson.

D

Today I am a happy man, but _____ 56 _____ was a hard day. Ivan, my sister's son, got _____ 57 _____ , and I was his best man. Like every best man before me, I had taken _____ 58 _____ of his rings, because it was up to me to hand them to Ivan at the right moment. But when the time came, I couldn't find the rings. Everyone at the church stared at me. I searched all my pockets, but couldn't find the rings. With all eyes on me, I started searching again. Everyone got more and more worried as I turned each pocket inside out. One had a penny in it. Another had a string. But none of them had a ring. I even took off my shoes and shook them out, but no rings fell out. The crowd was getting _____ 59 _____ , and I heard some of them begin to whisper. As I started to search my pockets for a third time, my _____ 60 _____ , Ivan, gave me an angry look. Sticking his hands in his pockets, he started tapping his foot. Then he stopped and, with a surprised look on his face, pulled the rings out of his own pocket. Now I ask you, why couldn't he have found the rings before everyone at church had gotten to see the hole in my left sock?

11

al li ga tor (al′ə gā′tər), a large reptile with a rather thick skin. It is like the crocodile but has a shorter and flatter head. Alligators live in the rivers and marshes of the warm parts of America and China. *noun.* [*Alligator* comes from Spanish words meaning "the lizard."]

ap pear ance (ə pir′əns), **1** act of coming in sight: *His appearance in the doorway was welcomed with shouts.* **2** coming before the public: *The singer made her first appearance in a concert in San Francisco.* **3** the way a person or thing looks: *I knew from his appearance that he was ill. noun.*

av e nue (av′ə nü *or* av′ə nyü), **1** a wide street. **2** road or walk bordered by trees. **3** way of approach: *Hard work is one avenue to success. noun.*

croc o dile (krok′ə dīl), a large reptile with a long body, four short legs, a thick skin, a pointed snout, and a long tail. Crocodiles live in the rivers and marshes of the warm parts of Africa, Asia, Australia, and America. *noun.*

cub (kub), a young bear, fox, or lion. *noun.*

dan ger ous (dān′jər əs), likely to cause harm; not safe; risky: *Shooting off firecrackers can be dangerous. adjective.*

de clare (di kler′ *or* di klar′), **1** say; make known: *Congress has the power to declare war. Travelers returning to the United States must declare the things which they bought abroad.* **2** say openly or strongly: *I declared that I would never do anything so foolish again. verb,* **de clared, de clar ing.**

ex per i ment (ek sper′ə ment *for 1;* ek sper′ə mənt *for 2*), **1** try in order to find out; make trials or tests: *Babies experiment with their hands. The painter is experimenting with different paints to get the color he wants.* **2** trial or test to find out something: *a cooking experiment. Scientists test out theories by experiment.* **1** *verb,* **2** *noun.*

lev el (lev′əl), **1** flat; even; having the same height everywhere: *a level floor.* **2** of equal height or importance: *The table is level with the sill of the window.* **3** something that is level. **4** instrument for showing whether a surface is level. **5** make level; put on the same level: *The builder leveled the ground with a bulldozer.* **6** raise and hold level for shooting; aim: *She leveled her rifle at the target.* **7** height: *The flood rose to a level of 60 feet.* **1,2** *adjective,* **3,4,7** *noun,* **5,6** *verb.*

nat ur al (nach′ər əl), **1** produced by nature; coming in the ordinary course of events: *natural feelings and actions, a natural death.* **2** not man-made or artificial: *Coal and oil are natural products.* **3** belonging to the nature one is born with: *It is natural for ducks to swim.* **4** in accordance with the facts of some special case: *a natural conclusion.* **5** like nature; true to life: *The picture looked natural.* **6** of or about nature: *the natural sciences.* **7** (in music) not changed in pitch by a sharp or a flat. **8** person who is especially suited for something because of inborn talent or ability: *He is a natural on the saxophone.* **1-7** *adjective,* **8** *noun.*

na ture (nā′chər), **1** the world; all things except those made by man: *the wonders of nature.* **2** the basic characteristic born in a person or animal and always present in a thing: *It is the nature of birds to fly.* **3** life without artificial things: *Wild animals live in a state of nature.* **4** what a person or thing really is; quality; character: *It is against her nature to be unkind.* **5** sort; kind: *books of a scientific nature. noun.*

par a graph (par′ə graf), **1** group of sentences that are about the same idea; distinct part of a chapter, letter, or composition. Paragraphs usually begin on a new line and are indented. **2** divide into paragraphs. **3** a separate note or item of news in a newspaper. **1,3** *noun,* **2** *verb.*

per son (pėr′sən), **1** man, woman, or child; human being: *Any person who wishes may come to the fair.* **2** the human body: *The person of the king was well guarded.* **3** bodily appearance: *He kept his person neat and trim. noun.*

in person, with or by one's own action or presence; personally: *Come in person; do not write or phone.*

sci en tist (sī′ən tist), person who has expert knowledge of some branch of science. Persons specially trained in and familiar with the facts and laws of such fields of study as biology, chemistry, mathematics, physics, geology, and astronomy are scientists. *noun.*

Sep tem ber (sep tem′bər), the ninth month of the year. It has 30 days. *noun.* [*September,* the Latin name for this month, came from a Latin word meaning "seven." The month was called this because it was the seventh month in the ancient Roman calendar.]

shark (shärk), a large and ferocious fish that eats other fish. Certain kinds are sometimes dangerous to human beings. *noun.*

shift (shift), **1** move or change from one place, position, or person, to another; change: *I shifted the heavy bag from one hand to the other. Don't try to shift the blame to someone else. The wind has shifted to the southeast.* **2** change of direction, position, or attitude: *a shift of the mind, a shift in policy.* **3** group of workers who work during the same period of time: *She is on the night shift this week.* **4** time during which such a group works. **5** manage to get along: *He left home at an early age and had to shift for himself.* **6** change the position of (the gears of an automobile). **1,5,6** *verb,* **2-4** *noun.*

sup port (sə pôrt′), **1** keep from falling; hold up: *Walls support the roof.* **2** give strength or courage to; keep up; help: *Hope supports us in trouble.* **3** provide for: *Parents usually support their children.* **4** be in favor of; back: *She supports the proposed law.* **5** help prove; bear out: *The facts support his claim.* **6** help; aid: *He needs the support of a scholarship.* **7** person or thing that supports; prop: *The neck is the support of the head.* **1-5** *verb,* **6,7** *noun.*

sur face (sėr′fis), **1** the outside of anything: *the surface of a mountain. An egg has a smooth surface.* **2** any face or side of a thing: *A cube has six surfaces. The upper surface of the plate has pictures on it.* **3** the outward appearance: *She seems rough, but you will find her very kind below the surface.* **4** of the surface; on the surface; having something to do with the surface: *a surface view.* **5** put a surface on; make smooth: *The town must surface this road.* **6** arise to the surface of the water: *The submarine surfaced.* **1-3** *noun,* **4** *adjective,* **5,6** *verb,* **sur faced, sur fac ing.**

vol ca no (vol kā′nō), mountain having an opening through which steam, ashes, and lava are forced out. *noun, plural* **vol ca noes** *or* **vol ca nos.** [*Volcano* comes from the Latin name of Vulcan, the Roman god of fire.]

Words in Sentences

Number from 1 to 20 on your answer sheet. Next to each numeral, write the word that belongs on that blank line in the sentence. Use the words at the left of each sentence. Use the Mini-Dictionary on the opposite page to find the meaning(s) of each word you don't know.

dangerous

shark

The great white ____1____ is perhaps the most ____2____ fish in the ocean.

experiment

nature

That ____3____ will help us to understand one of the laws of ____4____ .

declare

scientist

The ____5____ must ____6____ , in writing, the purpose of her work.

alligator

crocodile

appearance

The ____7____ of an ____8____ and a ____9____ is much the same, except for the shapes of their heads.

level

surface

support

Please help ____10____ the board so its ____11____ is ____12____ with the truck.

September

avenue

Those trees along the ____13____ begin to turn red in ____14____ .

natural

volcano

Few ____15____ forces are stronger than the force of a live ____16____ .

shift

cub

The bear ____17____ will be able to smell us if the wind begins to ____18____ .

paragraph

person

Can you write about that ____19____ in just one ____20____ ?

—— **Check your answers with the key.** ——

Number from 21 to 30 on your answer sheet. Next to each numeral, write the word from the box that completes the sentence.

alligator	nature
avenue	person
crocodile	scientist
cub	shark
experiment	volcano

B

Number from 31 to 40 on your answer sheet. Next to each numeral, write the word from the box that completes the group.

appearance	shift
declare	dangerous
September	paragraph
surface	support
natural	level

A

21. When I start my act, most other acts stop.
I don't really get angry, but I do blow my top!
I'm a _____ .

22. I'm the kind of child who wants to be free,
And there are no people in my family.
I'm a _____ .

23. I can live in America or China. It's all one to me.
When I float down a river, I look like a green tree.
I'm an _____ .

24. I'm sometimes found in Africa, so I'm not an alligator.
But I can take off your hand just as fast, and take off your arm later.
I'm a _____ .

25. I am you—whoever you may be.
You may be you, too. But still you are me!
I'm a _____ .

26. A force made me what I am today.
When everyone has gone, I'll go on the same way.
I am _____ .

27. To discover Mother Nature's laws, I always do my best.
I'm not Mother's teacher, but I do give her a test.
I'm a _____ .

28. Of all ways to discover, my way is the best.
You can't pass or fail me, but I am a kind of test.
I'm an _____ .

29. Sometimes I'm dirty; sometimes I'm neat.
I don't know why I'm not called just a "wide street."
I'm an _____ .

30. I can beat any other fish in a fight.
I can eat many things that swim with just one bite.
I'm a _____ .

—— **Check your answers with the key.** ——

B

31. beginning : start : : looks : _____
32. certain : sure : : flat : _____
33. patient : impatient : : safe : _____
34. lift : raise : : hold up : _____
35. person : Alice : : month : _____
36. loose : tight : : inside : _____
37. glance : look : : move sideways : _____
38. accident : accidental : : nature : _____
39. train : railroad car : : story : _____
40. question : ask : : fact : _____

—— **Check your answers with the key.** ——

Words in Stories

Before you do the Words in Stories exercise, take the *Spelling Recognition Test* on page 130 and check your answers with the key at the back of the book.

A

Number from 41 to 45 on your answer sheet. Next to each numeral, write the word from the box that completes the sentence.

support	experiment
paragraph	shark
scientist	

B

Number from 46 to 50 on your answer sheet. Next to each numeral, write the word from the box that completes the sentence.

dangerous	alligator
crocodile	appearance
declare	

C

Number from 51 to 55 on your answer sheet. Next to each numeral, write the word from the box that completes the sentence.

surface	volcano
September	level
shift	

D

Number from 56 to 60 on your answer sheet. Next to each numeral, write the word from the box that completes the sentence.

avenue	natural
person	cub
nature	

A

Several men and women who have studied animals believe that they can be trained to do almost anything. One ____41____ said that even a large, deadly fish like the ____42____ might be trained NOT to attack people. In a short ____43____, only twenty-five words long, she listed the facts that would ____44____ this idea. But she is still waiting to test her training plan. No one seems willing to get into the water with a "trained" shark and carry out the ____45____!

B

An ____46____ can be found only in the United States and China. It is an animal that lives in warm, fresh water and on land. Most people cannot tell it apart from a ____47____, which can be found in fresh and salty water in many parts of the world. The ____48____ of these two animals is so alike that only experts can tell one from the other, by the difference in their noses. One thing is safe to ____49____: If made angry, both of these animals can be ____50____ to humans. So, if you visit a warm place like Florida and come across one of these animals, give it the right of way.

C

In July, 1878, in a corn field in Mexico, the ground moved a little bit to the north. After that small ____51____ of the land, a thin crack appeared. The land to the north was a little higher now. The field was no longer quite ____52____, even though it looked much as it always had.

A month later, in that same spot, there was a large hill of dirt piled up on the ____53____. It has been forced up by something under it. Then, on ____54____ 28, 1878, a stream of melted rock, gas, and steam shot up into the air. The little crack in the earth had grown into a ____55____!

D

Wolves and dogs look much alike. It is only ____56____ for people to mistake a wolf ____57____ for a puppy when the young are born in the spring. But, by the fall of the year, the two animals are completely different. By then a young wolf can pull down and kill a deer. During the winter, if the food is scarce enough, young wolves in packs will even attack a ____58____.

A puppy raised as a pet near some safe street or even near an ____59____ could not stay alive for a month in the wild. And staying alive is the first law of ____60____.

— **Check your answers with the key.** —

ac ro bat (ak′rə bat), person who can swing on a trapeze, turn handsprings, walk a tightrope, or do other feats of bodily skill and strength. *noun.*

ad mire (ad mīr′), **1** look at or think of with wonder, pleasure, or satisfaction: *We all admired the beautiful painting.* **2** think highly of; respect: *Everyone admired the explorer's courage. verb,* **ad mired, ad mir ing.**

ad mit (ad mit′), **1** say (something) is real or true; acknowledge: *I admit now that I made a mistake.* **2** allow to enter: *She was admitted to law school. Windows admit light and air to the room. verb,* **ad mit ted, ad mit ting.**

art ist (är′tist), **1** person who paints pictures. **2** person who is skilled in any of the fine arts, such as sculpture, music, or literature. **3** person who does work with skill and good taste. *noun.*

com mit tee (kə mit′ē), group of persons appointed or elected to do some special thing: *Our teacher appointed a committee of five pupils to plan the class picnic. noun.*

con trol (kən trōl′), **1** have power or authority over; direct: *The government controls the printing of money.* **2** power; authority; direction: *Children are under their parents' control.* **3** hold back; keep down: *I was so upset by the accident that I couldn't control my tears.* **4** a holding back; a keeping down; restraint; check: *to lose control of one's temper.* **5** a device on or connected to a machine: *This control starts the dishwasher.* **6 the controls,** the instruments and devices by which an airplane, locomotive, or car is operated. 1,3 *verb,* **con trolled, con trol ling;** 2,4-6 *noun.*

de tec tive (di tek′tiv), **1** member of a police force or other person whose work is finding information secretly and solving crimes. **2** having something to do with detectives and their work: *She likes reading detective stories.* 1 *noun,* 2 *adjective.*

dis tance (dis′təns), **1** space in between: *The distance from the farm to the town is five miles.* **2** place far away: *She saw a light in the distance. noun.* **at a distance,** a long way: *The farm is at a distance from the railroad.* **keep at a distance,** refuse to be friendly or familiar with; treat coldly: *The teacher kept the students at a distance.*

ho tel (hō tel′), house or large building that supplies rooms and food for pay to travelers and others. *noun.*

ma gi cian (mə jish′ən), **1** person who can use magic: *The wicked magician cast a spell over the princess.* **2** person who entertains by magic tricks: *The magician pulled—not one, but three rabbits out of his hat! noun.*

mys ter i ous (mi stir′ē əs), **1** secret; hidden; hard to explain or understand: *Electricity is mysterious.* **2** suggesting mystery: *a mysterious look. adjective.*

mys ter y (mis′tər ē), **1** a secret; something that is hidden or unknown. **2** secrecy; obscurity. **3** something that is not explained or understood: *the mystery of the migration of birds. noun, plural* **mys ter ies.**

na tion al (nash′ə nəl), **1** of a nation; belonging to a whole nation: *national laws.* **2** citizen of a nation: *Many nationals of Canada visit the United States.* 1 *adjective,* 2 *noun.*

o bey (ō bā′), **1** do what one is told to do: *The dog obeyed and went home.* **2** follow the orders of: *You must obey the court's decision.* **3** yield to the control of: *A horse obeys the rein. verb.*

per fect (pėr′fikt *for 1,3-5, and 7;* pər fekt′ *for 2 and 6*), **1** having no faults; not spoiled at any point: *a perfect spelling paper, a perfect apple, a perfect life.* **2** remove all faults from; make perfect; add the finishing touches to: *perfect an invention. The artist was perfecting his picture.* **3** completely skilled; expert: *a perfect golfer.* **4** having all its parts there; complete: *The set was perfect; nothing was missing or broken.* **5** exact: *a perfect copy, a perfect circle.* **6** carry through; complete: *perfect a plan.* **7** entire; utter: *She was a perfect stranger to us.* 1,3-5,7 *adjective.* 2,6 *verb.*

pop u lar (pop′yə lər), **1** liked by most people: *a popular song.* **2** liked by acquaintances or associates: *His good nature makes him the most popular boy in the school.* **3** of the people; by the people; representing the people: *a popular election. The United States has a popular government.* **4** widespread among many people; common: *It is a popular belief that black cats bring bad luck.* **5** suited to the people: *popular prices, books on popular science. adjective.*

pri vate (prī′vit), **1** not for the public; for one person or a few special people: *a private road, a private house, a private letter.* **2** personal; not public: *the private life of a king, a private opinion. A diary is private.* **3** secret; confidential: *News reached her through private channels.* **4** having no public office: *a private citizen.* **5** soldier or marine of the lowest rank: *His brother was promoted from private to corporal last week.* 1-4 *adjective,* 5 *noun.* **in private,** secretly: *The rebels met in private to plot against the government.*

sev en teen (sev′ən tēn′), seven more than ten; 17. *noun, adjective.*

sev enth (sev′ənth), **1** next after the sixth: *Saturday is the seventh day of the week.* **2** one of seven equal parts: *A day is one seventh of a week. adjective, noun.*

up set (up set′ *for 1, 4, and 7;* up′set′ *for 2, 3, 5, 6, and 8*), **1** tip over; overturn: *I upset my glass of milk. Moving about in a boat may upset it.* **2** tipping over; overturn. **3** tipped over; overturned. **4** disturb greatly; disorder: *Rain upset our plans for a picnic. The bad news upset me.* **5** a great disturbance; disorder. **6** greatly disturbed; disordered: *an upset stomach.* **7** defeat unexpectedly in a contest: *The independent candidate upset the mayor in the election.* **8** an unexpected defeat: *The hockey team suffered an upset.* 1,4,7 *verb,* **up set, up set ting;** 2,5,8 *noun,* 3,6 *adjective.*

Words in Sentences

Number from 1 to 20 on your answer sheet. Next to each numeral, write the word that belongs on that blank line in the sentence. Use the words at the left of each sentence. Use the Mini-Dictionary on the opposite page to find the meaning(s) of each word you don't know.

__artist__   The light coming in from that window is ___1___

__perfect__   for the needs of an ___2___ .

__committee__   That ___3___ is only a short ___4___ from

__distance__   the building where the ___5___ meets.

__hotel__

__mystery__   It is a ___6___ why the bear cub didn't

__upset__   ___7___ the tent when he came to steal our food.

__acrobat__   The circus clown had to ___8___ that the

__admit__   ___9___ was more ___10___ than he was.

__popular__

__admire__   You have to ___11___ the way the ___12___

__control__   can ___13___ what the people see during a card

__magician__   trick.

__seventeen__   The captain thought the new ___14___ in his

__private__   company looked no older than ___15___ .

__seventh__   For some ___16___ reason, she gave a

__mysterious__   ___17___ of her money to her business school.

__national__   A ___18___ must learn and ___19___ city,

__detective__   state, and ___20___ laws.

__obey__

—— **Check your answers with the key.** ——

A

Number from 21 to 34 on your answer sheet. Next to each numeral, write the word from the box that completes the sentence.

obey	magician
admire	acrobat
seventh	artist
mystery	committee
distance	admit
hotel	seventeen
detective	control

B

Number from 35 to 40 on your answer sheet. Next to each numeral, write the word from the box that completes the sentence.

popular	private
perfect	upset
mysterious	national

A

21. He can't _____ his temper.
22. She turned _____ on her last birthday.
23. You should _____ the rules.
24. Does she _____ her mistakes?
25. Did they _____ the painting?
26. The _____ meets every Tuesday.
27. He came in _____ in the automobile race.
28. That _____ lost her brushes and paints.
29. The name of the unknown man is a deep _____ .
30. That _____ walks the high wire.
31. A long- _____ runner can run for miles.
32. That _____ does card tricks very well.
33. We stayed at a small and crowded _____ .
34. That _____ works on the police force.

—— **Check your answers with the key.** ——

B

35. wonder : wonderful : : nation : _____
36. tall : high : : strange : _____
37. freshly : fresh : : perfectly : _____
38. inquire : ask : : overturn : _____
39. general : captain : : captain : _____
40. coward : hero : : hated : _____

—— **Check your answers with the key.** ——

Before you do the Words in Stories exercise, take the *Spelling Recognition Test* on page 131 and check your answers with the key at the back of the book.

A

Number from 41 to 45 on your answer sheet. Next to each numeral, write the word from the box that completes the sentence.

distance	obey
mysterious	private
detective	

B

Number from 46 to 50 on your answer sheet. Next to each numeral, write the word from the box that completes the sentence.

mystery	popular
seventh	magician
acrobat	

C

Number from 51 to 55 on your answer sheet. Next to each numeral, write the word from the box that completes the sentence.

upset	control
perfect	admit
hotel	

D

Number from 56 to 60 on your answer sheet. Next to each numeral, write the word from the box that completes the sentence.

admire	national
seventeen	artist
committee	

A

Mike Moran made a business of learning other people's secrets. He was a good ____41____. Mike would spend hours or days following a person through the streets. When he was tailing a person, he always kept half a city block behind because he knew that was the best ____42____.

Sometimes Mike would tell people to give him information he needed. He was so big and mean-looking, most people were glad to ____43____. Mike always said his job was clear and easy to understand; there was nothing ____44____ about it. But Mike never talked much about particular things that he did. And he always kept his findings ____45____.

B

Ray always said he was really too old to enjoy magic tricks, but he liked watching El Topo, the great Spanish ____46____. Once, El Topo put a woman into a long wooden box and began to saw through the middle. At the ____47____ cut, the woman started to scream and kick her legs. Yet, when the box was opened, the woman was still in one piece. How she escaped the teeth of that saw was a ____48____ to Ray. It was easy to see why El Topo was so ____49____! Ray decided that the woman in the box was good too. To keep from being cut in half, she had had to move and turn as if she were a circus ____50____!

C

Kayko had to ____51____ that she had made a mistake. She had booked a room at a ____52____ called the El Dorado. The place had sounded ____53____. The price was right, and it was near the center of New York City. Kayko would be able to walk to her business meetings. But once she arrived, Kayko was told that the streets were not safe at night. Kayko was ____54____. How would she be able to get back to her room in the evenings? She did not have the money to get a room at another place. Kayko was stuck. Then she realized that, after all, there was a way to gain ____55____ over the danger. Every evening, after her meetings, Kayko stopped at a nearby shop that sells food and brings it to your door. She ordered her meal, waited until it was ready, and then ran alongside the man who bicycled the food to her place. She looked a little strange, running in her business clothes alongside a bicycle, but it got her safely to her room after dark.

D

A group of people in our city, ____56____ in all, agreed to work together to clean up the streets downtown. They all wanted Louisa Santini to be the chairperson of the ____57____.

Louisa was a strong woman and she had strong ideas about making the city beautiful again. She had an ____58____ paint pictures on the plain brick walls of the buildings. When people all over the country learned of her work, she was asked to become head of a ____59____ group. Louisa was a woman you had to ____60____ because she worked so hard for what she believed in.

—— **Check your answers with the key.** ——

19

Au gust (ô′gəst), the eighth month of the year. It has 31 days. *noun.* [*August* was named for Augustus, the first emperor of Rome. He lived from 63 B.C. to A.D. 14.]

a void (ə void′), keep away from; keep out of the way of: *We avoided driving through large cities on our trip. verb.*

cham pi on (cham′pē ən), **1** person, animal, or thing that wins first place in a game or contest: *a swimming champion. Her steer was the champion at the county fair last year.* **2** first; ahead of all others: *a champion runner. My sister is the champion reader in our house.* **1** *noun,* **2** *adjective.*

col lect (kə lekt′), **1** bring together; come together; gather together: *We collected sticks of wood to make a fire. I collect stamps as a hobby. Dust is collecting under the bed. A crowd soon collected at the scene of the accident.* **2** ask and receive pay for (debts, bills, dues, or taxes): *My scout troop collects dues each week. verb.*

col lec tion (kə lek′shən), **1** a bringing together; coming together: *The collection of these stamps took ten years.* **2** group of things gathered from many places and belonging together: *Our library has a large collection of books.* **3** money gathered from people: *A church takes up a collection to help pay its expenses.* **4** mass or heap: *a collection of dust under the bed. noun.*

con di tion (kən dish′ən), **1** state in which a person or thing is: *My room is in a messy condition.* **2** good condition; good health: *People who take part in sports must keep in condition.* **3** put in good condition: *Exercise conditions your muscles.* **4** social position; rank: *They were poor people of humble condition.* **5 conditions,** set of circumstances: *Icy roads cause bad driving conditions.* **6** thing on which something else depends; thing without which something else cannot be: *One of the conditions of the peace treaty was the return of all prisoners.* **7** accustom: *This dog was conditioned to expect food when it heard a bell.* **1,2,4-6** *noun,* **3,7** *verb.*

dam age (dam′ij), **1** harm or injury that lessens value or usefulness: *The accident did some damage to the car.* **2** harm or injure so as to lessen value or usefulness; hurt: *I damaged my sweater when I fell.* **1** *noun,* **2** *verb,* **dam aged, dam ag ing.**

de fend (di fend′), **1** keep safe; guard from attack or harm; protect: *The soldiers defended the fort.* **2** act, speak, or write in favor of: *The newspapers defended the governor's action. Lawyers are hired to defend people who are charged with crimes. verb.*

de mand (di mand′), **1** ask for as a right: *The prisoner demanded a trial.* **2** ask for with authority: *The teacher demanded the name of the student who rang the fire alarm.* **3** call for; require; need: *Training a puppy demands patience.* **4** claim: *Parents have many demands upon their time.* **5** desire and ability to buy: *Because of the large crop, the supply of apples is greater than the demand this year.* **1-3** *verb,* **4,5** *noun.*

de vel op (di vel′əp), **1** grow; bring or come into being or activity: *Plants develop from seeds. The seeds develop into plants. Scientists have developed many new drugs to fight disease. He developed an interest in collecting stamps. Swimming will develop many different muscles.* **2** work out in greater and greater detail: *Gradually we developed our plans for the club.* **3** treat (a photographic film or plate) with chemicals to bring out the picture. *verb.*

im i tate (im′ə tāt), **1** try to be like; follow the example of: *The little boy imitates his older brother.* **2** copy; make or do something like: *A parrot imitates the sounds it hears.* **3** act like: *He amused the class by imitating a duck, a monkey, and a bear.* **4** be like; look like: *Wood is sometimes painted to imitate stone. verb,* **im i tat ed, im i tat ing.**

im me di ate ly (i mē′dē it lē), **1** at once; without delay: *I answered his letter immediately.* **2** next; with nothing between. *adverb.*

in vent (in vent′), **1** make or think out (something new): *Alexander Graham Bell invented the telephone.* **2** make up: *Since they had no good reason for being late, they invented an excuse. verb.*

in ven tion (in ven′shən), **1** making something new: *the invention of gunpowder.* **2** thing invented: *Television is a modern invention.* **3** power of inventing: *An author must have invention to think up new ideas for stories.* **4** a made-up story; false statement: *That rumor is only an invention. noun.*

pro gram (prō′gram), **1** list of items or events set down in order with a list of the performers. There are concert programs, theater programs, and programs of a meeting. **2** items making up an entertainment: *The entire program was delightful.* **3** plan of what is to be done: *a school program, a business program, a government program. noun.*

rise (rīz), **1** get up from a lying, sitting, or kneeling position; stand up; get up: *Please rise from your seat when you recite.* **2** get up from sleep or rest: *I rise at 7 every morning.* **3** go up; come up: *The kite rises in the air. Bread rises. Mercury rises in a thermometer on a hot day. Fish rise to the surface.* **4** go higher; increase: *Butter rose five cents in price. The wind rose rapidly. My anger rose at that remark.* **5** going up; increase: *a rise in prices, the rise of a balloon.* **6** advance in importance or rank: *He rose from office clerk to president of the company.* **7** slope upward: *Hills rise in the distance.* **8** an upward slope: *The rise of the hill is gradual. The house is situated on a rise.* **9** come above the horizon: *The sun rises in the morning.* **10** start; begin: *The river rises from a spring. Quarrels often rise from trifles.* **11** origin; beginning: *the rise of a river, the rise of a storm, the rise of a new problem.* **12** become more cheerful; improve: *Our spirits rose at the good news.* **13** revolt; rebel: *The peasants rose against the nobles.* **1-4,6,7,9,10,12,13** *verb,* **rose, ris en, ris ing;** **5,8,11** *noun.*

give rise to, bring about; start; begin; cause: *Their sudden wealth gave rise to rumors about where the money came from.*

sixth (siksth), **1** next after the fifth. **2** one of six equal parts. *adjective, noun.*

strength (strengkth), **1** quality of being strong; power; force; vigor: *I do not have the strength to lift that heavy box. Steel is valued for its strength.* **2** degree of strength; intensity: *Some flavorings lose their strength in cooking. noun.*

on the strength of, relying on: *My parents bought me the dog on the strength of my promise to take care of it.*

twelfth (twelfth), **1** next after the 11th. **2** one of 12 equal parts. *adjective, noun.*

vic tor y (vik′tər ē), defeat of an enemy or opponent: *The game ended in a victory for our school. noun, plural* **vic tor ies.**

Words in Sentences

Number from 1 to 20 on your answer sheet. Next to each numeral, write the word that belongs on that blank line in the sentence. Use the words at the left of each sentence. Use the Mini-Dictionary on the opposite page to find the meaning(s) of each word you don't know.

collection	They should _____1_____ to know who did the _____2_____ to their record _____3_____ .
damage	
demand	

champion	If you want to win a _____4_____ , you should _____5_____ the person who is a _____6_____ .
imitate	
victory	

August	After our vacation in _____7_____ , we were in no _____8_____ to take another trip in September.
condition	

strength	If she is going to _____9_____ her track record, she will need all her _____10_____ .
defend	

twelfth	They expect to _____11_____ more than a _____12_____ of the money from their neighbors.
collect	

avoid	She had to _____13_____ a reason for being late to _____14_____ getting into trouble.
invent	

immediately	Almost _____15_____ after my aunt was offered a job, her hopes began to _____16_____ .
rise	

invention	He was the _____17_____ person who said the idea for the _____18_____ was his.
sixth	

develop	The new government _____19_____ will help small businesses _____20_____ .
program	

— **Check your answers with the key.** —

21. move up	_____
22. keep away from	_____
23. at once	_____
24. winner	_____
25. make up	_____
26. call for	_____
27. bring together	_____
28. state of	_____
29. made-up story	_____
30. be like	_____

—— **Check your answers with the key.** ——

A

Number from 21 to 30 on your answer sheet. Next to each numeral, write the word from the box that means about the **same** as the word(s) at the right.

invent	condition
demand	avoid
champion	invention
imitate	immediately
rise	collect

B

Number from 31 to 40 on your answer sheet. Next to each numeral, write the word from the box that completes the group.

August	program
damage	strength
defend	twelfth
develop	sixth
collection	victory

B

31. six : sixth : : twelve : _____
32. obey : command : : celebrate : _____
33. artist : painter : : force : _____
34. fight : box : : plan : _____
35. nine : eight : : September : _____
36. explain : explanation : : collect : _____
37. three : third : : six : _____
38. win : lose : : repair : _____
39. say : declare : : grow : _____
40. arrive : leave : : attack : _____

—— **Check your answers with the key.** ——

Before you do the Words in Stories exercise, take the *Spelling Recognition Test* on page 132 and check your answers with the key at the back of the book.

A

Number from 41 to 45 on your answer sheet. Next to each numeral, write the word from the box that completes the sentence.

demand	condition
strength	rise
champion	

B

Number from 46 to 50 on your answer sheet. Next to each numeral, write the word from the box that completes the sentence.

invent	imitate
develop	sixth
invention	

C

Number from 51 to 55 on your answer sheet. Next to each numeral, write the word from the box that completes the sentence.

immediately	collection
August	collect
program	

D

Number from 56 to 60 on your answer sheet. Next to each numeral, write the word from the box that completes the sentence.

avoid	twelfth
victory	defend
damage	

A

It didn't take long for Big Mike to move up in the boxing world. His speedy _____41_____ from club fights to main events amazed everyone.

But when Mike asked to fight for the boxing crown of the world, no one would listen. Mike began to _____42_____ his chance. His weight was down to 200 pounds and he was in top _____43_____. Finally they gave Mike a match for the boxing crown. He had the _____44_____ to beat the world _____45_____. And beat him Mike did.

B

Og was tired of carrying heavy loads on his back. He decided to _____46_____ a new and better way of moving things around. It wasn't easy, but finally, in his _____47_____ year of work, Og found the answer: the wheel! Og was sure all the people would want a wheel of their own. Some would try to _____48_____ him, but they would never be able to _____49_____ one as good as his. Everyone would have to buy his _____50_____!

C

Margaret Barclay had been asked to arrange a national flower show for early September. During the month of _____51_____ Margaret traveled everywhere, looking for people to take part.

In one town, she found someone who had gone to Africa to _____52_____ wild flowers. Margaret _____53_____ asked her to join the show. Ms. Barclay also found a man who dried flowers and pasted them into large books. She knew everyone would admire this beautiful _____54_____.

Just before the show, Margaret made a list of everything in the show and the names of those who were taking part. She sold this _____55_____ at the door for two dollars.

D

Lucy Goose and her Feathered Friends were attacked by the Barnyard Beasts on the _____56_____ of June. Lucy was able to _____57_____ her friends and even overcome the terrible Beasts, but each of the birds was harmed in some way.

Lucy studied the broken wings, the missing tail feathers, and the other _____58_____. "We have to stay away from the Beasts and _____59_____ these fights," she decided. "We might lose our lives if we win one more _____60_____ like this one!

——— Check your answers with the key. ———

Review Lesson

Choose the word from each pair that best completes the sentence.

A

1. mysterious	2. private
3. explanation	4. committee
5. yesterday	6. Tuesday
7. cub	8. alligator
9. shark	10. crocodile
11. fact	12. collection
13. enemy	14. scientist
15. information	16. program
17. August	18. twelfth
19. demand	20. defend
21. hotel	22. government
23. general	24. impatient
25. ancestors	26. envelope
27. argue	28. agree
29. command	30. declare
31. national	32. expert
33. realize	34. obey

B

35. collect	36. admit
37. habit	38. appearance
39. convenient	40. married
41. possession	42. invent
43. actually	44. familiar
45. hobby	46. purpose
47. experiment	48. September
49. beef	50. battery
51. develop	52. celebrate
53. particular	54. seventeen
55. person	56. surface
57. avenue	58. volcano
59. seventh	60. flare
61. business	62. discovery
63. popular	64. imitate
65. curiosity	66. invention

A

When the fish in the river suddenly began to die in a ___1 or 2___ way, a group of men and women got together to form a ___3 or 4___ to save them. Last ___5 or 6___ they marched on City Hall, carrying signs that said, "No to 'See you later, ___7 or 8___ ! After a while, ___9 or 10___ !' Give us clean water now!"

The city leaders told the group to learn the difference between ___11 or 12___ and feeling and said there was nothing wrong with the water. So the group found a ___13 or 14___ to test the water for them. They gathered enough ___15 or 16___ to prove that the water was dangerous to life.

One week later, on July ___17 or 18___ , the group was ready to ___19 or 20___ to see the leaders of the city ___21 or 22___ again. This time, the leaders said that the water would be cleaned up as soon as possible. "Try not to be so ___23 or 24___ ! Your ___25 or 26___ had clean water and your children will too," the group was told.

But the group of people didn't ___27 or 28___ with that. And they felt they had to ___29 or 30___ their ideas. "If you don't act now, we will hold statewide and ___31 or 32___ meetings. The law against killing is one law everyone must ___33 or 34___ ."

B

"I must ___35 or 36___ ," said Maria Valdez, "in ___37 or 38___ my Clean Machine is much like a toothbrush. But it is much more ___39 or 40___ , as you can see. Would you like to know how I came to ___41 or 42___ such a wonderful thing?

"One day, I started thinking about the ___43 or 44___ little tool we use to brush our teeth. I began to wonder why such a useful thing had only one ___45 or 46___ . So I began to ___47 or 48___ . First, I had to find out how to make the ___49 or 50___ watertight. Then I began to ___51 or 52___ brushes with different shapes and sizes, and I kept working until I had ___53 or 54___ !

"That was how I made my first Clean Machine. I tested it to make sure it would clean any ___55 or 56___ , even if it were full of holes. With my Clean Machine you can clean your teeth, your shoes, your clothing, or your windows! Just press the button and the soap shoots out of the brush like a little ___57 or 58___ ! And there's a ___59 or 60___ on the top which gives off so much light, you can work outdoors after dark.

"Now that I know how well the Clean Machine really works, I'm going into ___61 or 62___ to make more of them. Of course, I expect the big companies to ___63 or 64___ my little machine. But I'm not worried. I can always dream up a new ___65 or 66___ !"

Review Lesson

C

67. detective   68. acrobat
69. mystery   70. sixth
71. nephew   72. magician
73. opposite   74. dangerous
75. champion   76. artist
77. victory   78. death
79. rise   80. avoid
81. paragraph   82. distance
83. perfect   84. patient
85. damage   86. shift
87. instant   88. immediately
89. admire   90. hesitate
91. level   92. frozen
93. support   94. upset
95. strength   96. accident
97. control   98. condition
99. natural   100. nature

C

"Tito was born to fly," said Anna Pamplona, the sister of the famous circus ___67 or 68___ . Tito is the ___69 or 70___ in his family to want to sail through the air high above the floor of the Big Top. Tito himself is now training his little ___71 or 72___ to follow in his footsteps.

Like the rest of the family, Tito works without a net. But Tito's parents gave him a "net" of love and understanding while he was young. That's why Tito dares to try the most ___73 or 74___ tricks. He learned early to think he should be the best, a ___75 or 76___ among men.

"Tito faces ___77 or 78___ each time he does his circus act," Anna explained. "He must let go of his swing while it is still on the ___79 or 80___ . He has to spin through the air when his catcher is the right ___81 or 82___ away. Tito's timing must be ___83 or 84___ . If he were to ___85 or 86___ his weight just one ___87 or 88___ too soon, or ___89 or 90___ for even half a second, the swing would not be completely ___91 or 92___ when he let go. The catcher's arms would not be able to ___93 or 94___ Tito's weight and there would be a serious ___95 or 96___ . That's why Tito works every day to stay in top ___97 or 98___ . And that's how Tito makes it all look so easy. My brother, Tito Pamplona, makes it seem ___99 or 100___ for a person to fly!"

—— **Check your answers with the key.** ——

cheer ful (chir′fəl), **1** full of cheer; joyful; glad: *She is a smiling, cheerful girl.* **2** pleasant; bringing cheer: *This is a cheerful, sunny room.* **3** willing: *When my little brother wants to play he is not a very cheerful helper. adjective.*

crea ture (krē′chər), **1** any living person or animal: *We fed the lost dog because the poor creature was starving.* **2** anything created: *Ghosts are creatures of the imagination. noun.*

doz en (duz′n), 12; group of 12: *We had to have dozens of chairs for the party. We will need three dozen eggs and a dozen rolls. noun, plural* **doz ens** or *(after a number)* **doz en.**

dread ful (dred′fəl), **1** causing dread; terrible; fearful: *The fairy tale was about a dreadful dragon.* **2** very bad; very unpleasant: *I have a dreadful cold. adjective.*

fig ure (fig′yər), **1** symbol for a number. 1, 2, 3, 4, etc., are figures. **2** use numbers to find out the answer to some problem. **3** figures, arithmetic: *She is very good at figures.* **4** price: *The house was sold at a very high figure.* **5** Squares, triangles, cubes, and other shapes are called figures. **6** form or shape: *I could see the figure of a woman against the window.* **7** person; character: *The governor is a well-known figure throughout the state.* **8** stand out; appear: *The names of great leaders figure in the story of human progress.* **9** picture; drawing; diagram; illustration: *This book has many figures to help explain words.* **10** design or pattern: *the figures in the wallpaper. 1,3-7,9,10 noun, 2,8 verb,* **fig ured, fig ur ing.**

figure out, think out; understand: *Even the repairman couldn't figure out what had gone wrong with the washer.*

flick er (flik′ər), **1** shine or burn with a wavering, unsteady light: *The firelight flickered on the walls.* **2** a wavering, unsteady light or flame: *the flicker of an oil lamp.* **3** move lightly and quickly in and out, or back and forth: *We heard the birds flicker among the leaves.* **4** a quick, light movement: *the flicker of an eyelash. 1,3 verb, 2,4 noun.*

for tu nate (fôr′chə nit), **1** having good luck; lucky: *You are fortunate in having such a fine family.* **2** bringing good luck; having favorable results: *a fortunate occurrence. adjective.*

ghost (gōst), spirit of one who is dead appearing to the living: *The ghost of the murdered servant was said to haunt the house. noun.*

gloom y (glü′mē), **1** dark; dim: *a gloomy winter day.* **2** in low spirits; sad; melancholy: *a gloomy mood.* **3** dismal; causing gloom; discouraging: *There were gloomy predictions of a major earthquake. adjective,* **gloom i er, gloom i est.**

groan (grōn), **1** sound made down in the throat that expresses grief, pain, or disapproval; deep, short moan: *When I tried to wake her, she rolled over and with a groan went back to sleep.* **2** give a groan or groans: *The movers groaned as they lifted the piano. 1 noun, 2 verb.*

hor ri fy (hôr′ə fī), **1** cause to feel horror. **2** shock very much: *We were horrified by the wreck. verb,* **hor ri fied, hor ri fy ing.**

peace (pēs), **1** freedom from strife of any kind; condition of quiet, order, and security: *peace in the family.* **2** freedom from war: *work for world peace.* **3** agreement between enemies to end war: *sign the peace.* **4** quiet; calm; stillness: *peace of mind. We enjoy the peace of the country. noun.*

hold one's peace, keep still: *Do not speak when you should hold your peace.*

peace ful (pēs′fəl), **1** quiet; calm; full of peace: *It was peaceful in the mountains.* **2** liking peace; keeping peace: *peaceful neighbors. adjective.*

screech (skrēch), **1** cry out sharply in a high voice; shriek: *Someone screeched, "Help! Help!"* **2** a shrill, harsh scream or sound: *The screeches brought the police. 1 verb, 2 noun, plural* **screech es.**

shiv er (shiv′ər), **1** shake with cold or fear: *She crept shivering into bed.* **2** shaking from cold or fear. *1 verb, 2 noun.*

si lence (sī′ləns), **1** absence of sound or noise; stillness: *The teacher asked for silence.* **2** keeping still; not talking: *Silence gives consent.* **3** not mentioning: *Mother passed over his foolish remarks in silence.* **4** stop the noise of; make silent; quiet: *Please silence that barking dog. 1-3 noun, 4 verb,* **si lenced, si lenc ing.**

ter ror (ter′ər), **1** great fear: *The child has a terror of thunder.* **2** cause of great fear: *Pirates were once the terror of the sea. noun.*

thank ful (thangk′fəl), feeling thanks; grateful: *I am thankful for your help. adjective.*

van ish (van′ish), **1** disappear; disappear suddenly: *The sun vanished behind a cloud.* **2** pass away; cease to be: *Dinosaurs have vanished from the earth. verb.*

yell (yel), **1** cry out with a strong, loud sound: *I yelled with pain when the door slammed on my finger.* **2** a strong, loud cry. **3** say with a yell: *We yelled our good-bys to our friends as the bus moved away.* **4** a special shout or cheer used by a school or college at sports events. *1,3 verb, 2,4 noun.*

Words in Sentences

Number from 1 to 20 on your answer sheet. Next to each numeral, write the word that belongs on that blank line in the sentence. Use the words at the left of each sentence. Use the Mini-Dictionary on the opposite page to find the meaning(s) of each word you don't know.

ghost
silence
yell
They gave a loud ___1___ that broke the ___2___ when they saw the ___3___ moving closer.

peace
thankful
Everyone was ___4___ when the war was over and there was ___5___ once again.

horrify
creature
dreadful
The face of that ___6___ was so ___7___, it would ___8___ anyone.

flicker
gloomy
cheerful
When the rain fell, our ___9___ little campfire began to ___10___ and die down, and soon the whole world seemed dark and ___11___.

fortunate
peaceful
Isn't it ___12___ that we are living in ___13___ times?

groan
shiver
terror
It was ___14___ rather than the cold that made the trapped man give a low ___15___ and start to ___16___.

screech
dozen
When the cat crept too close, more than a ___17___ birds flew up into the tree, each one giving a loud ___18___.

figure
vanish
The ___19___ of a tall man could be seen walking through the forest until it passed behind a tree and seemed to ___20___.

—— **Check your answers with the key.** ——

A

Number from 21 to 30 on your answer sheet. Next to each numeral, write the word from the box that means about the **same** as the word(s) at the right.

yell	terror
dozen	fortunate
ghost	silence
peace	figure
gloomy	creature

B

Number from 31 to 34 on your answer sheet. Next to each numeral, write the word from the box that completes the sentence.

cheerful	dreadful
peaceful	thankful

C

Number from 35 to 40 on your answer sheet. Next to each numeral, write the word from the box that completes the sentence.

shiver	screech
horrify	groan
flicker	vanish

A

21. lucky _____
22. sad _____
23. shout _____
24. fear _____
25. spirit _____
26. calm _____
27. shape _____
28. living being _____
29. twelve _____
30. quiet _____

—— **Check your answers with the key.** ——

B

31. A creature from the deepest ocean might be _____.
32. A quiet country road in the summer might be _____.
33. A person who escaped from a burning house might be _____.
34. A children's play group might be _____.

—— **Check your answers with the key.** ——

C

35. fish : swim : : flame : _____
36. joy : smile : : fear : _____
37. cannon : blast : : alarm : _____
38. happy : upset : : laugh : _____
39. surface : appear : : disappear : _____
40. spark : sparkle : : horror : _____

—— **Check your answers with the key.** ——

Before you do the Words in Stories exercise, take the *Spelling Recognition Test* on page 133 and check your answers with the key at the back of the book.

Number from 41 to 45 on your answer sheet. Next to each numeral, write the word from the box that completes the sentence.

screech	flicker
vanish	yell
peace	

B

Number from 46 to 50 on your answer sheet. Next to each numeral, write the word from the box that completes the sentence.

dreadful	horrify
creature	silence
peaceful	

C

Number from 51 to 55 on your answer sheet. Next to each numeral, write the word from the box that completes the sentence.

thankful	dozen
fortunate	cheerful
gloomy	

Number from 56 to 60 on your answer sheet. Next to each numeral, write the word from the box that completes the sentence.

terror	figure
groan	ghost
shiver	

A

Jack and Doug were camping overnight for the first time. The night was black and silent. The campfire, which had been burning brightly, began to _____41_____ and die down. The boys edged closer to each other.

Suddenly a winged shape rose from a tree branch and gave a high _____42_____ of alarm. From behind a bush came a faint scratching sound. The frightened campers slowly turned. Was that a pair of eyes staring at them from the darkness? The shadowy figure crept away and then seemed to _____43_____ .

As they ran toward home, the boys began to _____44_____ loudly, filling the night with noise. As the sound died away, the little rabbit hopped out of the darkness to nibble at the boys' food in the _____45_____ and quiet of the forest.

B

Only one small being saw the spaceship when it landed. His _____46_____ nature made him trust the unknown. His curiosity made him rush toward it at top speed. He had time for one short scream before the mysterious gun cut him down. Then there was complete _____47_____ .

Now there was no one to carry the warning about the _____48_____ from outer space. The sight of it would certainly _____49_____ the others. It walked on only two legs. It had no wings at all, and it carried its head high on top of its _____50_____ , featherless body!

C

Lucky Duck lived near the quiet waters of Round Pond. "I'm such a _____51_____ bird," she would say in her loud, _____52_____ voice. "I've got plenty of food, a _____53_____ good friends, and a safe place to build my nest."

One day a group of campers forgot to put out their fire. It burned all the nesting places for miles around. "Well," said Lucky Duck, "at least I have my food and my friends. That's a lot to be _____54_____ for."

Next, a group of hunters came and blasted twelve birds out of the sky with their guns. "Well," said Lucky Duck, "I still have plenty of food left. In fact, there is more than enough food for one lonely, _____55_____ Lucky Duck like me!"

D

It was almost dark as Ray and Theresa walked carefully through the empty house. Outside, the winter wind was beginning to blow. Every so often there was a low _____56_____ that seemed to come from inside the walls of the house. Suddenly a door banged shut. In the distance a bird screeched. It could have been a person, screaming in _____57_____ !

At the top of the stairs a shadowy shape appeared. It was about the size and shape of a man's _____58_____ . Could it be a _____59_____ ? The room seemed deathly cold, and Theresa began to _____60_____ . "Let's buy it," she said. "Once we fix the cracks in the walls and put in some heat, this house will be a great place to live."

—— **Check your answers with the key.** ——

ache (āk), **1** continuous pain: *My cousin ate too much candy and got a stomach ache.* **2** suffer continuous pain; be in pain; hurt: *My arm aches.* **3** be eager; wish very much: *During the hot days of August we all ached to go swimming.* 1 *noun,* 2,3 *verb,* **ached, ach ing.**

breathe (brēᴛʜ), **1** draw air into the lungs and force it out. You breathe through your nose or through your mouth. **2** stop for breath; stop to rest after hard work or exercise: *Let's take a minute to breathe before we begin to work again.* **3** say softly; whisper: *Don't breathe a word of this to anyone.* **4** send out; give: *Her enthusiasm breathed new life into our club. verb,* **breathed, breath ing.**

cure (kyu̇r), **1** bring back to health; make well: *The medicine cured the sick child.* **2** get rid of: *cure a cold. Only great determination can cure a bad habit like smoking.* **3** remedy; something that removes or relieves disease or any bad condition: *a cure for a cold.* **4** preserve (bacon or other meat) by drying or salting. 1,2,4 *verb,* **cured, cur ing;** 3 *noun.*

dis ease (də zēz′), **1** sickness; illness; condition in which an organ, system, or part does not work properly: *People, animals, and plants can all suffer from disease. Cleanliness helps prevent disease.* **2** any particular illness: *Measles and chicken pox are two diseases of children. noun.*

doubt (dout), **1** not believe; not be sure; feel uncertain: *She doubted if we would arrive home on time.* **2** difficulty in believing: *Our faith helped overcome our doubt.* **3** an uncertain state of mind: *We were in doubt as to the right road.* 1 *verb,* 2,3 *noun.*

no doubt, certainly: *No doubt we will win.*

ex am i na tion (eg zam′ə nā′shən), **1** examining: *The doctor made a careful examination of my eyes.* **2** test: *an examination in arithmetic. noun.*

ex am ine (eg zam′ən), **1** look at closely and carefully: *The doctor examined the wound.* **2** test; test the knowledge or ability of; ask questions of: *The lawyer examined the witness. verb,* **ex am ined, ex am in ing.**

eye brow (ī′brou′), **1** hair that grows along the bony ridge just above the eye. **2** the bony ridge above the eye. *noun.*

eye lash (ī′lash′), **1** one of the hairs on the edge of the eyelid. **2** fringe of such hairs. *noun, plural* **eye lash es.**

eye lid (ī′lid′), the movable cover of skin, upper or lower, by means of which we can shut and open our eyes. *noun.*

health (helth), **1** being well or not sick; freedom from illness of any kind: *Rest, sleep, exercise, and cleanliness are important to your health.* **2** condition of the body or mind: *be in excellent health.* **3** a drink in honor of a person with a wish for that person's health and happiness. *noun.*

length (lengkth *or* length), **1** how long a thing is; what a thing measures from end to end; longest way a thing can be measured: *the length of your arm, eight inches in length.* **2** how long something lasts or goes on: *the length of a visit, the length of a book.* **3** distance: *The length of this race is one mile.* **4** a long stretch or extent: *Quite a length of hair hung down in a braid.* **5** something of a given length: *a length of rope, a dress length of silk. noun.*

at length, 1 at last: *At length, after many delays, the meeting started.* **2** with all the details; in full: *They told of their adventures at length.*

med i cine (med′ə sən), **1** substance, such as a drug, used to treat, prevent, or cure disease: *While I was sick I had to take my medicine three times a day.* **2** science of treating, preventing, or curing disease and improving health: *You must study medicine for several years before you can become a doctor. noun.*

nurse (nėrs), **1** person who takes care of the sick or the old, or is trained to do this: *Hospitals employ many nurses.* **2** be or act as a nurse for sick people; wait on or try to cure the sick. **3** cure or try to cure by care: *She nursed a bad cold by going to bed.* **4** woman who cares for and brings up the young children or babies of other persons. **5** act as a nurse; have charge of or bring up (another's baby or young child). **6** one who feeds and protects. **7** nourish; make grow; protect: *nurse a hatred in the heart, nurse a plant.* **8** treat with special care: *He nursed his sore arm by using it very little.* **9** give milk to (a baby) at the breast. **10** suck milk from the breast of a mother. 1,4,6 *noun,* 2,3,5,7-10 *verb,* **nursed, nurs ing.**

pain (pān), **1** a feeling of being hurt; suffering: *A cut gives pain. A toothache is a pain. The death of one we love causes us pain.* **2** cause to suffer; give pain: *Does your tooth pain you?* 1 *noun,* 2 *verb.*

take pains, be careful: *I took pains to write neatly.*

poi son (poi′zn), **1** a substance that is very dangerous to life and health when it is breathed or swallowed. Arsenic and lead are poisons. **2** kill or harm by poison. **3** put poison in or on: *poison food, poison arrows.* **4** anything deadly or harmful: *The poison of jealousy ended their friendship.* **5** have a very harmful effect on: *Lies poison the mind.* 1,4 *noun,* 2,3,5 *verb.*

pos si bly (pos′ə blē), **1** no matter what happens: *I cannot possibly go.* **2** perhaps: *Possibly you are right. adverb.*

stom ach (stum′ək), **1** the large muscular bag in the body which first receives the food, and digests some of it before passing it on to the intestines. **2** part of the body containing the stomach: *The ball hit me in the stomach.* **3** appetite. **4** put up with; bear; endure: *I cannot stomach violent movies.* **5** liking: *I have no stomach for killing harmless creatures.* 1-3,5 *noun,* 4 *verb.*

Wednes day (wenz′dē), the fourth day of the week; the day after Tuesday. *noun.* [*Wednesday* is from an earlier English word meaning "Woden's day." Woden was one of the most important of the old English gods.]

wound (wünd), **1** hurt or injury caused by cutting, stabbing, or shooting: *a knife wound, a bullet wound.* **2** injure by cutting, stabbing, or shooting; hurt: *The hunter wounded the deer.* **3** any hurt or injury to feelings or reputation: *Being fired from a job can be a wound to a person's pride.* **4** injure in feelings or reputation: *Their unkind words wounded me.* 1,3 *noun,* 2,4 *verb.*

Words in Sentences

Number from 1 to 20 on your answer sheet. Next to each numeral, write the word that belongs on that blank line in the sentence. Use the words at the left of each sentence. Use the Mini-Dictionary on the opposite page to find the meaning(s) of each word you don't know.

___doubt___
___eyebrow___

If you raise an ___1___ at something, people may think you ___2___ what is being said.

___pain___
___nurse___
___wound___

The ___3___ said my brother would feel little or no ___4___ from his ___5___ .

___Wednesday___
___examination___

Her history ___6___ is set for ten o'clock ___7___ morning.

___cure___
___possibly___
___disease___

How can they ___8___ find a ___9___ for every ___10___ during our lifetime?

___medicine___
___health___

The quickest way back to ___11___ is to take the right ___12___ .

___breathe___
___stomach___

It is very hard to ___13___ after you have been hit in the ___14___ .

___eyelash___
___length___

The shot missed me by only the ___15___ of an ___16___ !

___poison___
___ache___

He felt only a small ___17___ after the snake's ___18___ entered his body.

___examine___
___eyelid___

Alice added some light blue color to one ___19___ and looked in the mirror to ___20___ her work.

—— **Check your answers with key.** ——

A

Number from 21 to 24 on your answer sheet. Next to each numeral, write the word from the box that completes the sentence.

doubt	examine
ache	wound

B

Number from 25 to 31 on your answer sheet. Next to each numeral, write the word from the box that completes the sentence.

eyelash	disease
length	health
medicine	pain
eyebrow	

C

Number from 32 to 40 on your answer sheet. Next to each numeral, write the word from the box that completes the group.

stomach	examination
eyelid	breathe
Wednesday	cure
possibly	poison
nurse	

A

21. A tooth might _____ .
22. A knife might _____ .
23. A doctor might _____ .
24. A believer might _____ .

—— **Check your answers with the key.** ——

B

25. You can come down with a _____ .
26. You can swallow your _____ .
27. You can go running to build up your _____ .
28. You can lose an _____ .
29. You can use a ruler to find the _____ .
30. You can say "Ow!" to _____ .
31. You can raise an _____ .

—— **Check your answers with the key.** ——

C

32. cut : wound : : make well : _____ .
33. real : really : : possible : _____ .
34. water : drink : : air : _____ .
35. hair : head : : eyelash : _____ .
36. month : September : : day : _____ .
37. car : automobile : : test : _____ .
38. health : disease : : medicine : _____ .
39. door : room : : mouth : _____ .
40. school : teacher : : hospital : _____ .

—— **Check your answers with the key.** ——

Before you do the Words in Stories exercise, take the *Spelling Recognition Test* on page 134 and check your answers with the key at the back of the book.

A

Number from 41 to 45 on your answer sheet. Next to each numeral, write the word from the box that completes the sentence.

cure	nurse
examination	pain
eyelid	

B

Number from 46 to 50 on your answer sheet. Next to each numeral, write the word from the box that completes the sentence.

doubt	breathe
poison	wound
eyebrow	

C

Number from 51 to 55 on your answer sheet. Next to each numeral, write the word from the box that completes the sentence.

health	disease
ache	medicine
length	

D

Number from 56 to 60 on your answer sheet. Next to each numeral, write the word from the box that completes the sentence.

examine	Wednesday
possibly	stomach
eyelash	

A

Raylene's eye watered all the time. She went to the eye doctor for an _____41_____. "What is the trouble?" the doctor's nurse _____42_____ asked.

"I need new glasses," Raylene said. But the nurse wasn't so sure. She lifted Raylene's _____43_____ and removed a piece of dust.

"There, doesn't that feel better? And I didn't hurt you, did I?" asked the nurse. Raylene had to admit that she had felt no _____44_____ at all.

The doctor looked at Raylene's eye and put in some drops. "I'm glad the _____45_____ was that simple," Raylene thought.

B

Jackie Collins raised an _____46_____ as Val Dix explained why he had not done his homework. She knew that young man was trying to make a fool of her in front of the whole class. No one in the room believed Val Dix's story, but it was how she handled his excuse that would count. She told herself to _____47_____ deeply and speak calmly.

"Mr. Dix," said Jackie Collins coldly, "for someone who almost died just a few hours ago, you look to be very, very healthy. While I do not _____48_____ that you had trouble finishing your homework, I believe it was because you never started it, and not because of any _____49_____ in the wild berries you ate."

"Oh, Ms. Collins," cried Val, "your words _____50_____ me ever so badly."

"Oh my!" said Jackie Collins, startled. "I never meant to be less than kind. I will take back my words—and give you an F instead."

C

"I _____51_____ in every bone in my body," Martha Wingate told her friends. And in fact, Martha's _____52_____ had been failing for some time now. But she would not agree to enter a nursing home. "The name of my _____53_____ is simply old age," she said, "and in the _____54_____ of time I have left, I'm going to enjoy life. I want to travel. The best _____55_____ for me is to keep busy."

D

Bud went to _____56_____ Kootch for the twelfth time in as many minutes. He wiped a loose _____57_____ from the dog's face and wondered what _____58_____ could be wrong with his old friend. Every day for the past eight years, Kootch had met him at the door when he'd come home from work—every day except today. Today, Kootch just lay there, too deeply asleep even to hear his name being called.

It was only last week that the doctor had looked him over. Bud remembered the day well. It had been _____59_____, the day he had bought the used truck that he'd wanted and needed so badly. How happy he had been then. Now he couldn't be sadder. Feeling angry and sad at the thought that Kootch might be dying, Bud hit the table with his hand. That was when he noticed that the cake left over from yesterday's party was gone. He felt Kootch's _____60_____. Sure enough, it was full. Bud laughed. Kootch wasn't sick. He was just sleeping off a big, big meal.

33

ar e a (er′ē ə *or* ar′ē ə), **1** amount of surface; extent: *The area of this floor is 600 square feet.* **2** range of knowledge or interest: *Our science teacher is familiar with the areas of physics and chemistry.* **3** region: *The Rocky Mountain area is the most mountainous in the United States. noun.*

ar range ment (ə rānj′mənt), **1** a putting or a being put in proper order: *Careful arrangement of books in a library makes them easier to find.* **2** way or order in which things or persons are put: *You can make six arrangements of the letters A, B, and C.* **3** something arranged in a particular way: *a beautiful flower arrangement. This piece of music for the piano also has an arrangement for the violin.* **4 arrangements,** plans; preparations: *All arrangements have been made for our trip to Chicago. noun.*

brass (bras), **1** a yellowish metal that is made of copper and zinc. **2** anything made of brass, such as a band instrument, an ornament, or a dish: *I polished all the brass. noun, plural* **brass es.**

de part ment (di pärt′mənt), a separate part of some whole; special branch; division: *the toy department of a store. Our city government has a fire department and a police department. noun.*

flute (flüt), **1** a long, slender, pipelike musical instrument. A flute is played by blowing across a hole near one end. Different notes are made by covering different holes along its length with the fingers or with keys. **2** play on a flute. **3** sing or whistle so as to sound like a flute. 1 *noun,* 2,3 *verb,* **flut ed, flut ing.**

grade (grād), **1** class in school: *the fifth grade.* **2 the grades,** elementary school. **3** degree in rank, quality, or value: *The best grade of milk is grade A.* **4** group of persons or things having the same rank, quality, or value. **5** sort; place according to class: *These apples are graded by size.* **6** number or letter that shows how well one has done; mark: *My grade in English is B.* **7** give a mark or grade to: *The teacher graded the papers.* **8** slope of a road or railroad track: *a steep grade.* **9** make more nearly level: *The road up that steep hill was graded.* 1-4,6,8 *noun,* 5,7,9 *verb,* **grad ed, grad ing.**

gui tar (gə tär′), a musical instrument having six strings, played with the fingers or with a pick. *noun.*

im prove (im prüv′), **1** make better: *You could improve your writing if you tried.* **2** become better: *His health is improving.* **3** use well; make good use of: *We had two hours to wait and improved the time by seeing the city. verb,* **im proved, im prov ing.**

im prove ment (im prüv′mənt), **1** making better; becoming better: *Her schoolwork shows much improvement since last term.* **2** change or addition that adds value: *The improvements in our house were costly.* **3** person or thing that is better than a previous one; gain; advance: *Color television is an improvement over black-and-white television. noun.*

in stru ment (in′strə mənt), **1** thing used to do something; tool; mechanical device: *A forceps and a drill are two instruments used by dentists.* **2** device for producing musical sounds: *wind instruments, stringed instruments. A violin, cello, and piano were the instruments in the trio.* **3** thing with or by which something is done; person made use of by another; means: *The young king's wicked uncle used his influence as an instrument to gain power. noun.*

lip (lip), **1** either one of the two fleshy, movable edges of the mouth. **2** the folding or bent-out edge of any opening: *the lip of a pitcher. noun.*

mu sic (myü′zik), **1** art of making sounds that are beautiful, and putting them together into beautiful arrangements. **2** beautiful, pleasing, or interesting arrangements of sounds. **3** written or printed signs for tones: *Can you read music?* **4** any pleasant sound: *the music of a bubbling brook. We were made drowsy by the music of the wind blowing through the trees. noun.*

face the music, meet trouble boldly or bravely.

mu si cian (myü zish′ən), **1** person skilled in music. **2** person who sings or plays on a musical instrument, especially as a profession or business: *An orchestra is composed of many musicians. noun.*

pause (pôz), **1** stop for a time; wait: *I paused for a moment to look in a store window.* **2** a brief stop or rest: *After a pause for lunch we returned to work.* 1 *verb,* **paused, paus ing;** 2 *noun.*

per form (pər fôrm′), **1** do: *Perform your duties well.* **2** put into effect; carry out: *The surgeon performed an operation.* **3** act, play, sing, or do tricks in public. *verb.*

praise (prāz), **1** saying that a thing or person is good; words that tell the worth or value of a thing or person: *Everyone heaped praise upon the winning team.* **2** speak well of: *The coach praised the team for its fine playing.* **3** worship in words or song: *praise God.* 1 *noun,* 2,3 *verb,* **praised, prais ing.**

pro fes sor (prə fes′ər), teacher of the highest rank in a college or university. *noun.*

pu pil[1] (pyü′pəl), person who is learning in school or is being taught by someone. *noun.* [*Pupil*[1] comes from Latin words meaning "an orphan." Originally these words meant "a little boy" and "a little girl."]

pu pil[2] (pyü′pəl), the opening in the center of the eye which looks like a black spot. The pupil is the only place where light can enter the eye. *noun.* [*Pupil*[2] comes from a Latin word meaning "a little doll." The center of the eye was called this because when you look into the eye of another person you can see a tiny image of yourself.]

score (skôr), **1** record of points made in a game, contest, or test: *The score was 9 to 2 in favor of our school.* **2** make as points in a game, contest, or test: *score two runs in the second inning.* **3** keep a record of the number of points made in a game or contest: *The teacher will appoint some pupil to score for both sides.* **4** make as an addition to the score; gain; win: *She scored five runs for our team. See picture.* **5** group or set of twenty: *A score or more were present at the party.* **6** a written or printed piece of music arranged for different instruments or voices: *She was studying the score of the piece she was learning to play.* 1,5,6 *noun,* 2-4 *verb,* **scored, scor ing.**

settle a score, get even for an injury or wrong: *He had an old score to settle.*

trum pet (trum′pit), **1** a brass wind instrument that has a powerful tone, commonly a curved tube with a flaring bell at one end. **2** thing shaped like a trumpet. Ear trumpets were once used to help persons who were not able to hear well. **3** blow a trumpet. **4** a sound like that of a trumpet. **5** make a sound like a trumpet: *An elephant trumpeted.* **6** announce loudly or widely: *They trumpeted the news all over town.* 1,2,4 *noun,* 3,5,6 *verb.*

Words in Sentences

Number from 1 to 20 on your answer sheet. Next to each numeral, write the word that belongs on that blank line in the sentence. Use the words at the left of each sentence. Use the Mini-Dictionary on the opposite page to find the meaning(s) of each word you don't know.

grade
arrangement
improvement

Under the new _____1_____ with his parents, Paul can't go out on week-nights until his _____2_____ in English shows some _____3_____ .

music
area
flute

The air blown across the _____4_____ inside a _____5_____ makes the pleasant sound we call " _____6_____ ."

musician
professor

Nancy's _____7_____ said she would do well as either a singer or a _____8_____ .

guitar
instrument
pupil

A _____9_____ of mine who is studying the _____10_____ can also play another string _____11_____ .

lip
trumpet
perform

Paul will not be able to _____12_____ well on the _____13_____ until he develops more strength in his _____14_____ .

department
praise
brass

I brought the _____15_____ pot to Lacy's store to be fixed. I have only _____16_____ for that repair _____17_____ .

score
improve
pause

There was a _____18_____ in the game at half-time. Since the _____19_____ was 50 to 0 against us at that point, our coach said we could only _____20_____ .

—— **Check your answers with the key.** ——

A

Number from 21 to 30 on your answer sheet. Next to each numeral, write the word from the box that completes the sentence.

flute	department
improvement	music
brass	score
guitar	trumpet
pause	instrument

B

Number from 31 to 40 on your answer sheet. Next to each numeral, write the word from the box that completes the group.

lip	grade
professor	area
improve	perform
musician	arrangement
pupil	praise

A

21. An _____ is a kind of tool.
22. That _____ is a kind of metal.
23. A _____ is a kind of horn that can make music.
24. A _____ is a kind of stop.
25. That _____ is a kind of sound.
26. A _____ is a kind of record.
27. A _____ is a kind of pipe that can make music.
28. A _____ is a kind of part.
29. That _____ is a kind of change.
30. A _____ is a kind of box that can make music.

—— **Check your answers with the key.** ——

B

31. break : damage : : make better : _____
32. govern : government : : arrange : _____
33. magic : magician : : music : _____
34. piano : finger : : trumpet : _____
35. power : strength : : space : _____
36. command : order : : class : _____
37. book : read : : song : _____
38. imitate : copy : : speak well of : _____
39. mouth : lip : : eye : _____
40. cure : doctor : : teach : _____

—— **Check your answers with the key.** ——

Before you do the Words in Stories exercise, take the *Spelling Recognition Test* on page 135 and check your answers with the key at the back of the book.

Number from 41 to 45 on your answer sheet. Next to each numeral, write the word from the box that completes the sentence.

arrangement	praise
improvement	score
guitar	

Number from 46 to 50 on your answer sheet. Next to each numeral, write the word from the box that completes the sentence.

perform	trumpet
improve	brass
lip	

Number from 51 to 55 on your answer sheet. Next to each numeral, write the word from the box that completes the sentence.

pause	musician
instrument	music
area	

Number from 56 to 60 on your answer sheet. Next to each numeral, write the word from the box that completes the sentence.

Professor	grade
pupil	Department
flute	

A

More than playing in the rock-and-roll group, Chip Jordan liked writing his own songs. He was working hard on the _____41_____ for his newest song so that the whole group could play it at the next dance.

On a sheet of paper he wrote down the notes of music each person was to play. There was an _____42_____ for a _____43_____ or two, a piano, and the drums.

The song sounded great when it was played. Chip's friends couldn't _____44_____ him enough for the _____45_____ he'd made in the group's sound.

B

Like most of the people in the barnyard, Big Turk loved to march and play in the barnyard _____46_____ band. Turk was allowed to play the _____47_____ even though he wasn't very good. Everyone thought Turk's playing would have to _____48_____ since it could not possibly get worse. But then Turk fell and cut his _____49_____ the day before the big parade. He sounded much worse! Even so, Turk dressed up in his costume and marched along with the others. But he only pretended to play. Later, everyone said they had never heard Turk _____50_____ so well. He didn't make any music, but he didn't make any mistakes, either.

C

Rosalie just couldn't learn to read _____51_____ or play an _____52_____ . "Rosalie," one of her teachers asked, "why do you want to be a _____53_____ at all?"

After a rather long _____54_____ , Rosalie thought of an answer. "I know this must be the _____55_____ I belong in because I can't sing or paint pictures or even tap dance!"

D

Jules Abrams is in charge of the Music _____56_____ at the School of Fine Arts. But what he likes to do best is teach. He loves to be called " _____57_____ " instead of Mr. Abrams.

The people in his class learn to play the _____58_____ , but they must also learn to "play by the rules." Jules has each _____59_____ arrive five minutes early so that no class time is wasted waiting for latecomers. And he asks everyone to practice for 45 minutes each night. The _____60_____ Jules gives you is based in part on how well you obey the rules.

—— **Check your answers with the key.** ——

burst (bėrst), **1** open or be opened suddenly: *They burst the lock. The trees had burst into bloom.* **2** fly apart suddenly with force; explode: *If you stick a pin into a balloon, it will burst.* **3** go, come, or do by force or suddenly: *Don't burst into the room without knocking.* **4** be very full: *The barns were bursting with grain.* **5** bursting; outbreak: *There was a burst of laughter when the clown fell down.* **6** sudden display of activity or energy: *In a burst of speed, he won the race at the last minute.* 1-4 *verb,* **burst, burst ing;** 5,6 *noun.*

cus tom er (kus′tə mər), person who buys, especially a regular shopper at a particular store. *noun.*

De cem ber (di sem′bər), the 12th and last month of the year. It has 31 days. *noun.* [*December* came from a Latin word meaning "ten." In the ancient Roman calendar December was the tenth month of the year.]

earth quake (ėrth′kwāk′), a shaking or sliding of the ground, caused by the sudden movement of rock far beneath the earth's surface. *noun.*

en gi neer (en′jə nir′), **1** person who takes care of or runs engines. **2** person who is an expert in engineering. **3** guide; manage with skill: *She engineered the whole job from start to finish.* 1,2 *noun,* 3 *verb.*

e nor mous (i nôr′məs), very, very large; huge: *Long ago enormous animals lived on the earth.* *adjective.*

ex plode (ek splōd′), **1** blow up; burst with a loud noise: *The building was destroyed when the defective boiler exploded.* **2** cause to explode: *Some people explode firecrackers on the Fourth of July.* **3** burst forth noisily: *The speaker's mistake was so funny the audience exploded with laughter.* *verb,* **ex plod ed, ex plod ing.**

fi nal (fī′nl), **1** at the end; coming last: *The book was interesting from the first to the final chapter.* **2** deciding completely; settling the question: *The one with the highest authority makes the final decisions.* **3 finals,** the last or deciding set in a series of games or examinations. 1,2 *adjective,* 3 *noun.*

flood (flud), **1** fill to overflowing: *A wave flooded the holes I had dug in the sand.* **2** flow over: *The river flooded our fields.* **3** a great flow of water over what is usually dry land: *The heavy rains caused a serious flood near the river.* **4 the Flood,** (in the Bible) the water that covered the earth in the time of Noah. **5** a great outpouring of anything: *a flood of words.* **6** fill, cover, or overcome like a flood: *a room flooded with light.* 1,2,6 *verb,* 3-5 *noun.*

mid night (mid′nīt′), **1** twelve o'clock at night; the middle of the night. **2** of or like midnight. 1 *noun,* 2 *adjective.*

nec es sar y (nes′ə ser′ē), **1** needed; having to be done: *Was it necessary to fix the car engine? She flies when it is necessary to save time.* **2** that must be: *Death is a necessary end.* **3** thing impossible to do without: *Food, clothing, and shelter are necessaries of life.* 1,2 *adjective,* 3 *noun, plural* **nec es sar ies.**

news (nüz *or* nyüz), **1** something told as having just happened; information about something which has just happened or will soon happen: *The news that our teacher was leaving made us sad.* **2** report of a current happening or happenings in a newspaper or on television or radio. *noun.*

news pa per (nüz′pā′pər *or* nyüz′pā′pər), sheets of paper printed every day or week, telling the news, carrying advertisements, and having stories, pictures, articles, and useful information. *noun.*

noon (nün), 12 o'clock in the daytime; the middle of the day. *noun.*

or di nar y (ôrd′n er′ē), **1** usual; common; normal: *My ordinary lunch is soup, a sandwich, and milk.* **2** somewhat below the average: *The speaker was ordinary and tiresome. adjective.*
out of the ordinary, unusual; not regular: *Such a long delay is out of the ordinary.*

reg u lar (reg′yə lər), **1** fixed by custom or rule; usual: *Six o'clock was her regular hour of rising.* **2** following some rule or principle; according to rule: *A period is the regular ending for a sentence.* **3** coming again and again at the same time: *I make regular visits to the dentist.* **4** steady; habitual: *A regular customer trades often at the same store.* **5** well-balanced; even in size, spacing, or speed: *regular teeth, regular breathing.* **6** orderly; methodical: *He leads a regular life.* **7** properly fitted or trained: *The regular cook in our cafeteria is sick.* **8** member of a regularly paid group of any kind: *The fire department was made up of regulars and volunteers.* 1-7 *adjective,* 8 *noun.*

re port (ri pôrt′), **1** account of something seen, heard, or read about. **2** anything formally expressed, generally in writing: *a school report.* **3** give or bring an account of; make a report of; state formally: *Our treasurer reports that all dues are paid up.* **4** repeat (what one has heard or seen); bring back an account of; describe; tell: *The radio reports the news and weather. The divers reported the treasures they had found in the sunken ship.* **5** present oneself: *Report for work at eight o'clock.* **6** sound of a shot or an explosion: *the report of a gun.* 1,2,6 *noun,* 3-5 *verb.*

shel ter (shel′tər), **1** something that covers or protects from weather, danger, or attack: *Trees are a shelter from the sun.* **2** protect; shield; hide: *shelter runaway slaves.* **3** protection; refuge: *We took shelter from the storm in a barn.* 1,3 *noun,* 2 *verb.*

si ren (sī′rən), kind of whistle that makes a loud, piercing sound. *noun.*

thrift y (thrif′tē), careful in spending; economical; saving: *a thrifty shopper. adjective,* **thrift i er, thrift i est.**

Words in Sentences

Number from 1 to 20 on your answer sheet. Next to each numeral, write the word that belongs on that blank line in the sentence. Use the words at the left of each sentence. Use the Mini-Dictionary on the opposite page to find the meaning(s) of each word you don't know.

engineer
flood

The ____1____ who had built the old bridge said it would be unsafe if there should be another ____2____ .

news
shelter
report

There was a special ____3____ on the evening ____4____ that told us how to reach the nearest ____5____ on high ground.

noon
earthquake
December

On ____6____ 21, we had one large ____7____ , followed by several smaller ones, all between 11 A.M. and ____8____ .

enormous
explode
newspaper

The ____9____ stated that there were several ____10____ tanks of gas behind the apartment building, which were sure to ____11____ during a fire.

regular
midnight
necessary

If the ____12____ firefighters can't finish the job by ____13____ , it will be ____14____ to bring in more help.

final
customer
thrifty

The radio announcer said that each ____15____ would receive a free gift during the ____16____ day of the store's ____17____ holiday sale.

siren
ordinary
burst

The unmarked police car looked quite ____18____ until the officer placed the special ____19____ on the roof and drove off in a ____20____ of speed.

—— **Check your answers with the key.** ——

A

Number from 21 to 28 on your answer sheet. Next to each numeral, write the word from the box that completes the sentence.

shelter	noon
earthquake	thrifty
midnight	news
burst	newspaper

B

Number from 29 to 36 on your answer sheet. Next to each numeral, write the word from the box that means about the **same** as the word(s) at the right.

flood	enormous
ordinary	necessary
explode	regular
report	final

C

Number from 37 to 40 on your answer sheet. Next to each numeral, write the word from the box that completes the group.

December	siren
customer	engineer

A

21. If it is _____ , it is the middle of the night.

22. If it is _____ , it is important to many people.

23. If it is _____ , it is time for lunch.

24. If it is a _____ that has printed the story, the facts have been carefully checked.

25. If it is an _____ that is shaking the building, you had better lie flat on the floor.

26. If you need _____ from the sun, you should wear a large hat.

27. If you hear a _____ of laughter, someone has been telling a good joke.

28. If it is _____ to save string so you don't have to buy it, then it would also make sense to save paper bags.

—— **Check your answers with the key.** ——

B

29. blow up _____
30. very large _____
31. needed _____
32. steady _____
33. last _____
34. cover with water _____
35. usual _____
36. state or tell _____

—— **Check your answers with the key.** ——

C

37. music : flute : : noise : _____
38. sixth : twelfth : : June : _____
39. car : driver : : train : _____
40. hospital : patient : : store : _____

—— **Check your answers with the key.** ——

Before you do the Words in Stories exercise, take the *Spelling Recognition Test* on page 136 and check your answers with the key at the back of the book.

A

Number from 41 to 45 on your answer sheet. Next to each numeral, write the word from the box that completes the sentence.

flood	explode
enormous	burst
earthquake	

B

Number from 46 to 50 on your answer sheet. Next to each numeral, write the word from the box that completes the sentence.

ordinary	siren
news	noon
final	

C

Number from 51 to 55 on your answer sheet. Next to each numeral, write the word from the box that completes the sentence.

midnight	customer
thrifty	regular
December	

D

Number from 56 to 60 on your answer sheet. Next to each numeral, write the word from the box that completes the sentence.

shelter	engineer
newspaper	report
necessary	

A

The greatest danger during an _____41_____ doesn't come from the sudden shift in the earth's surface. The problems develop when water pipes _____42_____ and _____43_____ streets and buildings all over the city. Also, cracks develop in the gas pipe lines, allowing pools of gas to collect. If there is a spark nearby, this gas will _____44_____ and cause any number of _____45_____ fires.

B

Tuesday was the _____46_____ day of the stock car races. By _____47_____ , most of the town was out at the track. The _____48_____ business in town had stopped until a winner was declared.

Around three in the afternoon we heard the scream of a _____49_____ and saw a police car speeding on its way to the track. This could only mean some bad _____50_____ . We all knew the chances the drivers took to win that prize money.

C

"Calling all _____51_____ shoppers!" read the full-page ad in the July 30 paper. "Free gifts to each _____52_____ ! The B.B. Wolf Company is having another **BIG** sale you can't afford to miss! We've taken fifty dollars off the _____53_____ price of all TVs and record players!"

You had to look closely to see the small print at the bottom of the ad. It read: "This special offer is good only during the second Wednesday in _____54_____ , between the hours of _____55_____ and 12:15 A.M."

D

During the terrible snowstorm last week, the snow was so heavy that drivers couldn't see the road ahead. It was _____56_____ for them to pull over and stop. Several people died in the storm after they left their cars to find _____57_____ .

A woman came from a big city _____58_____ to write a special _____59_____ on driver safety. She asked Carl Anders, who works as a safety _____60_____ for the highway department, to help her write it. Carl said it was important for people to know that a car offers them the most safety when they are caught out in a snowstorm, far from help. The car is warm, dry, and easy for searchers to find in the snow.

—— **Check your answers with the key.** ——

41

an cient (ān′shənt), **1** belonging to times long past: *In Egypt, we saw the ruins of an ancient temple built six thousand years ago.* **2 the ancients,** people who lived long ago, such as the ancient Greeks, Romans, and Egyptians. 1 *adjective,* 2 *noun.*

as tro naut (as′trə nôt), pilot or member of the crew of a spacecraft. *noun.* [*Astronaut* comes from Greek words meaning "star sailor."]

flight[1] (flīt), **1** act or manner of flying: *the flight of a bird through the air.* **2** distance a bird, bullet, or airplane can fly. **3** group of things flying through the air together: *a flight of pigeons.* **4** trip in an aircraft. **5** airplane that makes a scheduled trip: *She took the three o'clock flight to Boston.* **6** soaring above or beyond the ordinary: *a flight of the imagination.* **7** set of stairs from one landing or one story of a building to the next. *noun.*

flight[2] (flīt), running away; escape: *The flight of the prisoners was discovered. noun.*

in ter rupt (in′tə rupt′), **1** break in upon (talk, work, rest, or a person speaking); hinder; stop: *A fire drill interrupted the lesson.* **2** break in: *It is not polite to interrupt when someone is talking. verb.*

Jan u ar y (jan′yü er/ē), the first month of the year. It has 31 days. *noun.* [*January* comes from Janus, the ancient Roman god of gates and doors and of beginnings and endings. He was shown with two faces, one looking forward and one looking backward.]

mil lion (mil′yən), one thousand thousands; 1,000,000. *noun, adjective.*

mod ern (mod′ərn), **1** of the present time; of times not long past: *Color television is a modern invention.* **2** up-to-date; not old-fashioned: *modern views. adjective.*

nine teen (nīn′tēn′), nine more than ten; 19. *noun, adjective.*

ninth (nīnth), **1** next after the eighth. **2** one of nine equal parts. 1 *adjective,* 1,2 *noun.*

or bit (ôr′bit), **1** path of the earth or any one of the planets about the sun. **2** path of any heavenly body about another heavenly body. **3** path of an artificial satellite around the earth. **4** travel around the earth or some other heavenly body in an orbit: *Some artificial satellites can orbit the earth in less than an hour.* 1-3 *noun,* 4 *verb.*

plan et (plan′it), one of the heavenly bodies that move around the sun. Mercury, Venus, the earth, Mars, Jupiter, Saturn, Uranus, Neptune, and Pluto are planets. *noun.* [*Planet* comes from Greek words meaning "wandering stars." People of ancient times thought of the planets as stars that moved about while the other stars stayed in one place.]

plat form (plat′fôrm), **1** a raised level surface: *There is a platform beside the track at the railroad station. The hall has a platform for speakers.* **2** plan of action or statement of beliefs of a group: *The platform of the new political party demands lower taxes. noun.*

prep a ra tion (prep′ə rā′shən), **1** preparing; making ready: *I sharpened the knife in preparation for carving the meat.* **2** being ready. **3** thing done to get ready: *He made thorough preparations for his trip by carefully planning which way to go.* **4** a specially made medicine or food or mixture of any kind: *The preparation included camphor. noun.*

pro tect (prə tekt′), shield from harm or danger; shelter; defend; guard: *Protect yourself from danger. Protect the baby's eyes from the sun. verb.*

pro tec tion (prə tek′shən), **1** act of protecting; condition of being kept from harm; defense: *We have a large dog for our protection.* **2** thing or person that prevents damage: *A hat is a protection from the sun. noun.*

rock et (rok′it), **1** device consisting of a tube open at one end in which an explosive or fuel is rapidly burned. The burning explosive or fuel creates gases that escape from the open end and force the tube and whatever is attached to it upward or forward. Some rockets, such as those used in fireworks displays, shoot into the air and burst into showers of sparks. Larger rockets are used in weapons of war and to send spacecraft beyond the earth's atmosphere. **2** go like a rocket; move very, very fast: *The singing group rocketed to fame with its first hit record. The racing car rocketed across the finish line to victory.* 1 *noun,* 2 *verb.*

soar (sôr), **1** fly at a great height; fly upward: *The eagle soared without flapping its wings.* **2** rise beyond what is common and ordinary: *Prices are soaring. Her hopes soared when she was called in for a job interview. verb.*

sug gest (səg jest′), **1** bring to mind; call up the thought of: *The thought of summer suggests swimming, tennis, and hot weather.* **2** put forward; propose: *She suggested a swim, and we all agreed.* **3** show in an indirect way; hint: *His yawns suggested that he would like to go to bed. verb.*

tel e scope (tel′ə skōp), **1** an instrument for making distant objects appear nearer and larger. The stars are studied by means of telescopes. **2** force together, one inside another, like the sliding tubes of some telescopes: *When the two railroad trains crashed into each other, the cars were telescoped.* **3** be forced together in this way. 1 *noun,* 2,3 *verb,* **tel e scoped, tel e scop ing.**

zer o (zir′ō), **1** the figure 0: *There are three zeros in 40,006.* **2** point marked as 0 on the scale of a thermometer. **3** temperature that corresponds to 0 on the scale of a thermometer. **4** of or at zero: *The other team's score was zero.* **5** nothing. **6** not any; none at all: *The weather station at the airport announced zero visibility.* **7** a very low point: *The team's spirit sank to zero after its fifth defeat in a row.* 1-3,5,7 *noun, plural* **zer os** or **zer oes;** 4,6 *adjective.*

Words in Sentences

Number from 1 to 20 on your answer sheet. Next to each numeral, write the word that belongs on that blank line in the sentence. Use the words at the left of each sentence. Use the Mini-Dictionary on the opposite page to find the meaning(s) of each word you don't know.

rocket

orbit

astronaut

In 1961 a Russian _____1_____ blasted off from earth on top of a _____2_____ and became the first person in history to _____3_____ the earth.

flight

preparation

During the 1960s there was a great deal of _____4_____ for the first space _____5_____.

telescope

platform

In the years to come, a space station will have a huge _____6_____ and other instruments carefully set up on a _____7_____ where scientists will work.

suggest

protection

modern

If you want _____8_____ against fires in your home, I would _____9_____ you buy a _____10_____ smoke alarm that signals when there is smoke in the room.

interrupt

nineteen

By the age of _____11_____ most young people would like to _____12_____, or stop, their lessons for a while.

zero

protect

We must_____13_____ the men and women on the spaceship if trouble develops just before the countdown reaches _____14_____, the lift-off stage.

ancient

soar

To _____15_____ through the air with perfect control and then travel to the moon and the stars is an _____16_____ dream shared by all peoples.

ninth

planet

The spaceship *Pioneer 10* has passed Pluto, which is the _____17_____ and the farthest _____18_____ from the Sun.

January

million

Although our sun is only 93 _____19_____ miles (150,000,000 kilometers) away, the distance from earth to the next star is 4.3 light years. That means that the light from the star that you see in April started out four years earlier, in _____20_____.

—— **Check your answers with the key.** ——

A

Number from 21 to 24 on your answer sheet. Next to each numeral, write the word from the box that completes the sentence.

interrupt	suggest
protection	preparation

B

Number from 25 to 31 on your answer sheet. Next to each numeral, write the word from the box that completes the sentence.

million	astronaut
platform	telescope
zero	orbit
rocket	

C

Number from 32 to 40 on your answer sheet. Next to each numeral, write the word from the box that completes the group.

flight	January
modern	planet
nineteen	ninth
protect	ancient
soar	

A

21. If you buy a guard dog for _____ , you must be sure it is well trained.

22. If you _____ me one more time, I won't tell you the end of the story.

23. If you _____ often enough that people are not telling the truth, they may decide to tell you lies.

24. If you begin to work without enough _____ , you may not be able to finish the job.

—— **Check your answers with the key.** ——

B

25. A _____ has a blast-off stage.
26. An _____ took a trip to the moon.
27. A _____ is a raised surface.
28. A _____ helps you see things that are far away.
29. A planet's _____ has its sun in the center.
30. A _____ stands for nothing.
31. A _____ has seven figures.

—— **Check your answers with the key.** ——

C

32. hesitate : pause : : defend : _____
33. automobile : airplane : : ride : _____
34. twenty : nineteen : : February : _____
35. enter : leave : : dive : _____
36. the sun : star : : earth : _____
37. very bad : terrible : : very old : _____
38. dangerous : safe : : ancient : _____
39. eight : nine : : eighteen : _____
40. July : September : : seventh : _____

—— **Check your answers with the key.** ——

Before you do the Words in Stories exercise, take the *Spelling Recognition Test* on page 137 and check your answers with the key at the back of the book.

Number from 41 to 45 on your answer sheet. Next to each numeral, write the word from the box that completes the sentence.

astronaut	platform
telescope	preparation
million	

B

Number from 46 to 50 on your answer sheet. Next to each numeral, write the word from the box that completes the sentence.

protection	flight
planet	orbit
nineteen	

Number from 51 to 55 on your answer sheet. Next to each numeral, write the word from the box that completes the sentence.

modern	ninth
zero	interrupt
January	

D

Number from 56 to 60 on your answer sheet. Next to each numeral, write the word from the box that completes the sentence.

soar	ancient
protect	suggest
rocket	

A

After years of _____41_____ at the Space Control Center, the _____42_____ team was able to put together a huge _____43_____ above the space station. Here, scientists would make use of a new kind of _____44_____ to collect information from a mysterious star that was only 500 _____45_____ miles away.

B

The following is the report of Captain Ryan of the spaceship *Silver Moon:* "We have discovered a rather small, blue and white _____46_____ far from our own. There is enough gas on the surface of this heavenly body to give us _____47_____ from the more deadly rays of its yellow sun.

"If we change the direction of our present _____48_____, we can reach the planet in only _____49_____ of their days. We should be able to complete an _____50_____ around it in a half hour and then land. It looks like it might be a nice place to call 'home.'"

C

Hank hung up the telephone and immediately went to Maria's desk. "I hate to _____51_____ your work," he said, "but Jo Enos's young boy, Lenny, is missing. He and his friend Syed went into the woods. Lenny found some raccoon tracks and was following them deeper into the woods when Syed got hungry and left him. The police are asking everyone to look for the boy. I thought maybe you and Brandy could help, especially since it has started snowing and the boys' tracks will soon be covered."

Maria had been training her dog, Brandy, for search and rescue work. He was new to it, but they might as well give it a try. "I'll run home and get Brandy," Maria said. "Ask the police to get some of the boy's clothes for Brandy to smell."

Fifteen minutes later, Brandy and Maria were making their way through the woods. It was the _____52_____ day of the month, and the month was _____53_____. It was cold outdoors, not much above _____54_____ even during the day. Soon the sun would set and it would get a lot colder still. "Brandy," said Maria, "If you don't find Lenny in the next hour, there's little chance we'll ever find him alive." The dog just smelled the air and pulled Maria deeper into the woods.

When the light started to fail, Maria had to face the truth. It was time to turn back. She knew the boy would not live through the night in this cold weather, but neither would she and Brandy if full darkness trapped them there. Even in this _____55_____ day and age, there was no way to find a boy at night in the deep woods. With a heavy heart Maria ordered, "Brandy, home!"

Brandy did not listen. He gave a bark and pulled her forward. She knew then that he had picked up the boy's scent. She radioed the others the news, then started calling the boy's name as she walked forward. Before long, a small voice in the distance answered: Lenny!

D

The _____56_____ was invented about a thousand years ago by the Chinese people. This _____57_____ invention was used as a toy to celebrate holidays. It probably made a fine show as it lifted off the ground to _____58_____ fifty or sixty feet overhead.

As far as we know, the German people were the first to _____59_____ that this "toy" could be made large enough to _____60_____ a country from attack and even to carry people to the planets. The idea of using rockets to soar to outer space was first thought of about a hundred years ago.

Review Lesson

Choose the word from each pair that best completes the sentence.

A

1. flute	2. astronaut
3. report	4. flight
5. ancient	6. ordinary
7. medicine	8. poison
9. disease	10. examination
11. enormous	12. possibly
13. pain	14. midnight
15. orbit	16. flicker
17. health	18. screech
19. planet	20. dreadful
21. soar	22. horrify
23. vanish	24. rocket
25. telescope	26. creature
27. peace	28. instrument
29. ghost	30. suggest
31. cure	32. examine
33. protection	34. professor

B

35. arrangement	36. eyelid
37. perform	38. interrupt
39. music	40. eyelash
41. December	42. preparation
43. shiver	44. doubt
45. platform	46. grade
47. ache	48. stomach
49. cheerful	50. ninth
51. pupil	52. guitar
53. pause	54. lip
55. brass	56. final

A

At first no one back on earth was worried when the ____1 or 2____ team failed to call in. But when Control Center still had not received a ____3 or 4____ three hours later, the experts began to worry. This was the first ship to travel all the way out into deep space, and anything out of the ____5 or 6____ could mean it was having trouble. When the TV picture from the spaceship finally began to come through, Control Center knew it had big trouble on its hands.

The captain stated that the ship had run into a cloud of either dust or gas. She was afraid that the cloud was some kind of ____7 or 8____ , but she couldn't say why she thought that. Everyone on board was terribly afraid, although they didn't know what they were frightened of. They felt as though they had caught a strange, new ____9 or 10____ . They heard voices and saw things that couldn't ____11 or 12____ be there. But they felt no ____13 or 14____ , just a terrible fear.

As she was talking, the captain herself grew more and more afraid. Then something seemed to pass in front of the screen. The picture went out, came back, then started to ____15 or 16____ . Control Center heard a loud ____17 or 18____ . Now the cloud grew thicker. It seemed to have a ____19 or 20____ power. When the picture of the captain and the spaceship returned, the experts saw something that would ____21 or 22____ anyone. The captain and the spaceship were as clear as glass! You could see right through them. And then they seemed to ____23 or 24____ !

It was impossible! Control Center knew the ship must be out there somewhere. But their most powerful ____25 or 26____ could not find it. In fact, no ____27 or 28____ on earth was able to track it down. It seemed as though the first ship to travel into deep space had become a ____29 or 30____ ship !

Control Center continued to ____31 or 32____ the skies, looking for the lost ship. And other spaceships continued to blast off at the planned times, but they did not head all the way out into deep space. Something terrible was out there. And no power on earth could offer any ____33 or 34____ against it.

B

Nina sat backstage in her dressing room and added more eye shadow to each ____35 or 36____ . In three minutes she would step out in front of the crowd and ____37 or 38____ . Nina had been working night and day on her ____39 or 40____ . She would soon see whether all her ____41 or 42____ would make her a star. Nina began to worry. She started to ____43 or 44____ that she was good enough to make the ____45 or 46____ with the experts who were there tonight.

"Ms. Watkins!" someone called. "You're on!" Nina had a tight feeling in her ____47 or 48____ . But she gave a bright, ____49 or 50____ smile and stepped out onto the stage.

At the end of the first song, the soft sound of the ____51 or 52____ died away. Nina was to ____53 or 54____ and then hit the ____55 or 56____ high note and hold it, all alone. When the last note died away, there was complete

Review Lesson

_____57 or 58_____ . Then the crowd went wild! There were shouts of "More! More!"

At last the show was over. Nina waited for each early morning _____59 or 60_____ to go on sale. What would the experts say about her singing? She could hardly _____61 or 62_____ as she opened the first paper. One writer noted, "Ms. Watkins was in great form tonight. Don't miss hearing her!" Another writer stated, "When Nina Watkins calmed down this evening, her singing showed much _____63 or 64_____ . I think she'll become a great star!"

The writers went on to _____65 or 66_____ her, but Nina had read enough. She tried to act as usual, but inside she felt very _____67 or 68_____ . Her hard work had indeed paid off!

C

To Carlos Sanchez and the rest of the town, _____69 or 70_____ morning was just a _____71 or 72_____ day. Then they heard the nine o'clock _____73 or 74_____ . Miles away, under the sea, there had been a giant _____75 or 76_____ which formed a huge "killer" wave on the surface of the Pacific Ocean. In about three hours that wave would reach their island! It would rush across the beach and sweep up the river to _____77 or 78_____ the small town.

Like almost everyone else in town, Carlos worked in the large plant owned by the Santos family. Carlos had been to school where he studied to become an _____79 or 80_____ . He knew that the people in the town were in great danger. Carlos told them it would be _____81 or 82_____ for everyone to leave the town immediately and get to high ground.

Mr. Santos, the owner of the plant, didn't agree with Carlos. He didn't think that the wave would travel that far up the river and told everyone to stay on the job. Carlos argued with his boss until it was almost _____83 or 84_____ , when the wave was due to arrive. Then he left, taking as many people as he could to safety.

The killer wave came rushing up the narrow river just as Carlos had said it would. It crashed against the buildings, sweeping away trees and buildings under the rushing wall of dirty water. It was too late to _____85 or 86_____ the buildings or the people inside.

When the water level finally dropped and Carlos hurried back, he saw a scene of _____87 or 88_____ . Thank goodness the Red Cross had flown in workers to help. A _____89 or 90_____ was busy caring for Mr. Santos, who had a small _____91 or 92_____ near his _____93 or 94_____ .

"This is a terrible thing that has happened," Mr. Santos told Carlos in a _____95 or 96_____ tone of voice. "There will be more than a _____97 or 98_____ dollars' worth of damage!" Santos said nothing about the people who had died following his orders. Carlos, ready to _____99 or 100_____ with anger, looked at his boss. But Carlos' mouth remained closed. He turned and walked angrily away.

—— **Check your answers with the key.** ——

buck (buk), **1** a male deer, goat, hare, or rabbit. **2** jump into the air with the back curved and come down with the front legs stiff: *My horse began to buck, but I managed to stay on.* **3** throw by bucking: *The cowboy was bucked by the bronco.* **4** charge against; work against: *The swimmer bucked the current with strong strokes.* **1** *noun,* **2-4** *verb.*

buck le (buk′əl), **1** catch or clasp used to hold together the ends of a belt, strap, or ribbon. **2** fasten together with a buckle: *She buckled her belt.* **3** a metal ornament for a shoe. **4** bend; wrinkle: *The heavy snowfall caused the roof of the shed to buckle.* **5** a bend or wrinkle. **1,3,5** *noun,* **2,4** *verb,* **buck led, buck ling.**

buckle down to, work hard at: *I buckled down to my studies before the test.*

cor ral (kə ral′), **1** pen for horses, cattle, and other animals. **2** drive into or keep in a corral: *The cowhands corralled the herd of wild ponies.* **3** hem in; surround; capture: *The reporters corralled the mayor and began asking questions.* **1** *noun,* **2,3** *verb,* **cor ralled, cor ral ling.**

dif fi cult (dif′ə kult), **1** hard to do or understand: *Arithmetic is difficult for some pupils.* **2** hard to manage; hard to please: *My cousins are difficult and always want things their own way.* *adjective.*

dis grace (dis grās′), **1** loss of honor or respect; shame: *The disgrace of being sent to prison was hard for them to bear.* **2** loss of favor or trust: *The king's former adviser is now in disgrace.* **3** cause disgrace to; bring shame upon: *The traitor disgraced his family and friends.* **4** person or thing that causes dishonor or shame: *The slums in many cities are a disgrace.* **1,2,4** *noun,* **3** *verb,* **dis graced, dis grac ing.**

gal lop (gal′əp), **1** the fastest gait of a horse or other four-footed animal. In a gallop, all four feet are off the ground together at each leap. **2** ride at a gallop: *The hunters galloped after the hounds.* **3** go or cause to go at a gallop: *The wild horse galloped off. We galloped our horses down the road.* **4** go very fast; hurry: *gallop through a book.* **1** *noun,* **2-4** *verb.*

hitch (hich), **1** fasten with a hook, ring, rope, or strap: *She hitched her horse to a post.* **2** a fastening; catch: *Our car has a hitch for pulling a trailer.* **3** kind of knot used to fasten a rope to a post or to some other object for a short time. **4** move or pull with a jerk: *He hitched his chair nearer to the fire.* **5** a short, sudden pull or jerk: *He gave his pants a hitch.* **6** obstacle; stopping: *A hitch in their plans made them miss the train.* **1,4** *verb,* **2,3,5,6** *noun,* *plural* **hitch es.**

hu man (hyü′mən), **1** of persons; that people have: *Kindness is a human trait. To know what will happen in the future is beyond human power.* **2** of or having the form or qualities of people: *Men, women, and children are human beings. Those monkeys seem almost human.* **3** person; human being. **1,2** *adjective,* **3** *noun.* [*Human* comes from a Latin word meaning "of man" or "of human beings."]

in sist (in sist′), keep firmly to some demand, some statement, or some position: *He insists that he had a right to use his brother's tools. She insists that we should all learn to ski.* *verb.*

mare (mer *or* mar), a female horse or donkey. *noun.*

pants (pants), a two-legged outer garment reaching from the waist to the ankles or sometimes to the knees; trousers. *noun plural.*

ro de o (rō′dē ō *or* rō dā′ō), a contest or exhibition of skill in roping cattle or riding horses and steers. *noun, plural* **ro de os.**

rough (ruf), **1** not smooth; not level; not even: *rough boards, the rough bark of oak trees, a rough, rocky hill.* **2** stormy: *rough weather, a rough sea.* **3** likely to hurt others; harsh; not gentle: *rough manners.* **4** without luxury and ease: *He led a rough life at his summer camp.* **5** without polish or fine finish: *rough diamonds.* **6** not completed; done as a first try; without details: *a rough drawing, a rough idea.* **7** coarse and tangled: *rough fur, a dog with a rough coat of hair.* **8** unpleasant; hard; severe: *She had a rough time in the hospital.* **9** make rough; roughen: *A strong wind roughed up the waves.* **10** shape or sketch roughly: *rough out a plan, rough in the outlines of a face.* **11** roughly: *Those older boys play too rough for me.* **1-8** *adjective,* **9,10** *verb,* **11** *adverb.*

rough it, live without comforts and conveniences: *They have been roughing it in the woods this summer.*

sad dle (sad′l), **1** seat for a rider on a horse's back, on a bicycle, or on other like things. **2** thing shaped like a saddle. A ridge between two mountain peaks is called a saddle. **3** put a saddle on: *Saddle the horse.* **4** burden: *to be saddled with too much work.* **1,2** *noun,* **3,4** *verb,* **sad dled, sad dling.**

in the saddle, in a position of control.

sleeve (slēv), part of a garment that covers the arm. *noun.*

sta ble¹ (stā′bəl), **1** building where horses or cattle are kept and fed: *She took riding lessons at the stable.* **2** group of animals housed in such a building: *a stable of race horses.* **3** put or keep in a stable. **1,2** *noun,* **3** *verb,* **sta bled, sta bling.**

sta ble² (stā′bəl), not likely to move or change; steadfast; firm; steady: *Concrete reinforced with steel is stable. The world needs a stable peace.* *adjective.*

stal lion (stal′yən), a male horse that can father young. *noun.*

stead y (sted′ē), **1** changing little; uniform; regular: *He is making steady progress at school.* **2** firmly fixed; firm; not swaying or shaking: *This post is steady as a rock. Hold the ladder steady.* **3** not easily excited; calm: *steady nerves.* **4** having good habits; reliable: *He is a steady young man.* **5** make steady; keep steady: *Steady the ladder while I climb to the roof.* **6** become steady: *Our sails filled as the wind steadied from the east.* **1-4** *adjective,* **stead i er, stead i est; 5,6** *verb,* **stead ied, stead y ing.**

tame (tām), **1** taken from the wild state and made obedient: *a tame bear.* **2** gentle; without fear: *The birds are so tame that they will eat from our hands.* **3** make tame; break in: *The lion was tamed for the circus.* **4** become tame: *White rats tame easily.* **5** deprive of courage; tone down; subdue: *The bad news tamed our spirits.* **6** dull: *The party was tame because we were sleepy.* **1,2,6** *adjective,* **tam er, tam est; 3-5** *verb,* **tamed, tam ing.**

wear y (wir′ē), **1** tired: *weary feet, a weary brain.* **2** tiring: *a weary wait.* **3** make or become weary; tire: *Walking all day wearied the tourists.* **1,2** *adjective,* **wear i er, wear i est; 3** *verb,* **wear ied, wear y ing.**

Words in Sentences

Number from 1 to 20 on your answer sheet. Next to each numeral, write the word that belongs on that blank line in the sentence. Use the words at the left of each sentence. Use the Mini-Dictionary on the opposite page to find the meaning(s) of each word you don't know.

human

buck

stallion

As soon as he felt a ___1___ on his back, the wild ___2___ would put down his head and, kicking out with his legs, start to ___3___ .

hitch

steady

corral

Mary Beth chose two ___4___ horses from the group in the ___5___ and started to ___6___ them to the wagon.

gallop

insist

mare

Chuck should not ___7___ that the gray ___8___ run any faster unless he wants to see her ___9___ .

disgrace

difficult

rodeo

It is so ___10___ to ride one of the wild bulls at the ___11___ that it is no ___12___ to be thrown.

sleeve

pants

rough

Even a young calf can play ___13___ . The winner of the calf-roping contest had his shirt ___14___ pulled off and got dust all over the seat of his ___15___ .

buckle

saddle

It took two men to hold the wild horse while Jim lifted the ___16___ onto the animal's back and began to ___17___ it in place.

stable

tame

weary

The horse was too ___18___ to fight anymore when Jim finally rode her back to the ___19___ for the night. For now, at least, she was ___20___ .

—— **Check your answers with the key.** ——

A

Number from 21 to 28 on your answer sheet. Next to each numeral, write the word from the box that means about the **opposite** of the word(s) at the right.

tame	steady
weary	insist
hitch	disgrace
rough	difficult

B

Number from 29 to 35 on your answer sheet. Next to each numeral, write the word from the box that completes the sentence.

buck	buckle
stallion	saddle
stable	sleeve
corral	

C

Number from 36 to 40 on your answer sheet. Next to each numeral, write the word from the box that completes the group.

gallop	pants
rodeo	mare
human	

A

21. smooth _____
22. easy _____
23. honor _____
24. wild _____
25. unfasten _____
26. give in _____
27. not regular _____
28. lively _____

—— **Check your answers with the key.** ——

B

29. A _____ is a kind of seat.
30. A _____ is a pen for animals.
31. A _____ is a kind of jump.
32. A _____ is a kind of shelter.
33. A _____ covers the arm.
34. A _____ is a kind of catch.
35. A _____ is a kind of horse.

—— **Check your answers with the key.** ——

C

36. acrobat : circus : : cowboy : _____
37. arm : sleeve : : leg : _____
38. man : woman : : stallion : _____
39. person : run : : horse : _____
40. stable : animal : : house : _____

—— **Check your answers with the key.** ——

Before you do the Words in Stories exercise, take the *Spelling Recognition Test* on page 138 and check your answers with the key at the back of the book.

A

Number from 41 to 45 on your answer sheet. Next to each numeral, write the word from the box that completes the sentence.

buck	buckle
saddle	rodeo
stallion	

B

Number from 46 to 50 on your answer sheet. Next to each numeral, write the word from the box that completes the sentence.

stable	gallop
mare	insist
tame	

C

Number from 51 to 55 on your answer sheet. Next to each numeral, write the word from the box that completes the sentence.

hitch	pants
rough	sleeve
weary	

D

Number from 56 to 60 on your answer sheet. Next to each numeral, write the word from the box that completes the sentence.

Steady	human
corral	difficult
disgrace	

A

Tom felt he was a little too old to enter the _____41_____ this year, but he really needed the prize money. And, as it happened, Tom's first ride was on an unusually mean _____42_____ . As soon as the beast felt Tom's weight in the _____43_____ , he dropped his head, kicked out with his legs, and began to _____44_____ wildly. Somehow, Tom hung on until, at one point, the horse reared up and fell backwards. Tom was able to walk away. When the horse tried to stand, one of his legs was so weak, it started to _____45_____ . It was the last ride for them both.

B

"Are you sure these horses are _____46_____ ?" Marcie asked the man who ran the riding _____47_____ . The man had to _____48_____ that all the horses were friendly and gentle before Marcie would choose one. She picked a two-year-old _____49_____ that seemed nice and calm.

For a time the horse walked along quietly, with Marcie holding on for dear life. Suddenly the animal began to pick up speed. "Whoa!" Marcie shouted. "Nice horsie!" The horse just ran faster until finally she broke into a _____50_____ on the way home.

"I said they were friendly and gentle," the man explained afterwards. "You didn't ask if they liked to obey orders!"

C

Sam had been working for over an hour this morning and already he was tired. When the bucket of cool water was passed to him, the _____51_____ boy took a long drink and wiped his mouth on his _____52_____ . Sam was living with his aunt and uncle this summer and today he was sanding the floors of their farmhouse to help earn his keep. In a minute, he'd have to _____53_____ up his heavy work _____54_____ and get back on the job.

"Time's a-wasting, boy," his uncle said. "It's nearly eight o'clock. Smooth down that _____55_____ spot in the corner and we'll get breakfast!"

D

John "Horse" Fly had lived all his life in and around the big ranch, but so far he had not once been on horseback. "If a _____56_____ being can do it, I can too," John told his friends. "Riding horses can't be all that _____57_____ ."

So John flew over to the _____58_____ and jumped onto one of the horses. The animal immediately tried to give John the brush-off with its huge tail. "_____59_____ there, fellow," John called. "Take it easy, now!" That only made the horse jump and twist harder. John became frightened and flew away.

"I'm sorry," he told his friends. "I'm a _____60_____ to the Fly name."

"Come with us," his friends told him. "We'll attack that horse together."

—— **Check your answers with the key.** ——

ac cuse (ə kyüz′), charge with being or doing something bad: *The driver was accused of speeding.* verb, **ac cused, ac cus ing.**

ar rest (ə rest′), **1** seize by authority of the law; take to jail or court: *The police arrested the burglar.* **2** a stopping; seizing: *We saw the arrest of the burglar.* **3** stop; check: *Filling a tooth arrests decay.* **4** catch and hold: *Our attention was arrested by a strange sound.* 1,3,4 *verb,* 2 *noun.*

cap ture (kap′chər), **1** make a prisoner of; take by force, skill, or trick: *We captured butterflies with a net.* **2** person or thing taken in this way: *Captain Jones's first capture was an enemy ship.* **3** a capturing or a being captured: *The capture of this ship took place on July 6.* **4** attract and hold; catch and keep: *The story of Alice in Wonderland captures the imagination.* 1,4 *verb,* **cap tured, cap tur ing;** 2,3 *noun.*

court (kôrt), **1** space partly or wholly enclosed by walls or buildings: *The four apartment houses were built around a court of grass.* **2** short street. **3** place marked off for a game: *a tennis court, a basketball court.* **4** place where a king, queen, or other ruler lives; royal palace. **5** household and followers of a king, queen, or other ruler: *The court of Queen Elizabeth I was noted for its splendor.* **6** ruler and his or her advisers as a governing body or power: *An order of the Court of St. James's is an order of the British government.* **7** assembly held by a king, queen, or other ruler: *The queen held court to hear from her advisers.* **8** place where justice is administered: *The prisoner was brought to court for trial.* **9** persons who administer justice; judge or judges: *The court found him guilty.* **10** assembly of such persons to administer justice: *Several cases await trial at the next court.* **11** seek the favor of; try to please: *The nobles courted the king to get positions of power.* **12** try to win the love of; pay loving attention to in order to marry: *He courted her by bringing her flowers every day.* **13** try to get; seek: *It is foolish to court danger.* 1-10 *noun,* 11-13 *verb.*

e qual (ē′kwəl), **1** the same in amount, size, number, value, or rank: *Ten dimes are equal to one dollar. All persons are considered equal before the law.* **2** be the same as: *Four times five equals twenty.* **3** person or thing that is equal: *In spelling she had no equal.* **4** make or do something equal to: *Our team equaled the other team's score, and the game ended in a tie.* 1 *adjective,* 2,4 *verb,* 3 *noun.*
equal to, strong enough for: *One horse is not equal to pulling a load of five tons.*

fist (fist), a tightly closed hand: *He shook his fist at me. noun.*

free dom (frē′dəm), **1** being free. **2** liberty; power to do, say, or think as one pleases. **3** free use: *We gave our guest the freedom of the house.* **4** too great liberty: *I dislike his freedom of manner.* **5** ease of movement or action: *A fine athlete performs with freedom. noun.*

jail (jāl), **1** prison, especially one for persons awaiting trial or being punished for some small offense. **2** put in jail; keep in jail: *The police arrested and jailed the suspected thief.* 1 *noun,* 2 *verb.*

nerv ous (nėr′vəs), **1** of the nerves: *a nervous disorder, nervous energy.* **2** easily excited or upset: *A person who has been overworking is likely to become nervous.* **3** restless or uneasy; timid: *Are you nervous about staying alone at night? adjective.*

pris on (priz′n), **1** a public building in which criminals are confined: *The convicted killer was sentenced to prison for life.* **2** any place where a person or animal is shut up unwillingly: *The small apartment was a prison to the big dog. noun.*

pris on er (priz′n ər), **1** person who is under arrest or held in a jail or prison. **2** person who is kept shut up unwillingly, or who is not free to move. **3** person taken by the enemy in war. *noun.*

quar rel (kwôr′əl), **1** an angry dispute; fight with words: *The children had a quarrel over the division of the candy.* **2** fight with words; dispute or disagree angrily: *The two friends quarreled and now they don't speak to each other.* **3** cause for a dispute: *A bully likes to pick quarrels.* **4** find fault: *It is useless to quarrel with fate, because one does not have control over it.* 1,3 *noun,* 2,4 *verb.*

shoul der (shōl′dər), **1** part of the body to which an arm, foreleg, or wing is attached. **2** part of a garment that covers a shoulder. **3 shoulders,** the two shoulders and the upper part of the back: *The man carried a trunk on his shoulders.* **4** bear (a burden or blame): *She shouldered the responsibility of sending her niece through college.* **5** something that sticks out like a shoulder: *Don't drive on the shoulder of the road.* **6** push with the shoulders: *She shouldered her way through the crowd.* 1-3,5 *noun,* 4,6 *verb.*

shove (shuv), **1** push; move forward or along by force from behind: *Help me shove this bookcase into place.* **2** push roughly or rudely against; jostle: *The people shoved to get on the crowded car.* **3** push: *We gave the boat a shove which sent it far out into the water.* 1,2 *verb,* **shoved, shov ing;** 3 *noun.*

steal (stēl), **1** take something that does not belong to one; take dishonestly: *Robbers stole the money.* **2** take, get, or do secretly: *She stole time from her lessons to read a story.* **3** take, get, or win by artful or charming ways: *The baby stole our hearts.* **4** move secretly or quietly: *She had stolen softly out of the house.* **5** in baseball, run to second, third, or home base, as the pitcher throws the ball to the catcher. **6** act of stealing. 1-5 *verb,* **stole, sto len, steal ing;** 6 *noun.*

sto len (stō′lən). See **steal.** *The money was stolen by a thief. verb.*

sur ren der (sə ren′dər), **1** give up; give (oneself or itself) up; yield: *The captain had to surrender to the enemy. As the storm got worse, we surrendered all hope of going camping. We surrendered ourselves to sleep.* **2** act of surrendering: *The surrender of the fort came at dawn.* 1 *verb,* 2 *noun.*

sus pect (sə spekt′ *for 1-3;* sus′pekt *for 4*), **1** imagine to be so; think likely: *The old fox suspected danger and did not touch the trap. I suspect that they have been delayed.* **2** believe guilty, false, or bad without proof: *The police suspected them of being thieves.* **3** feel no confidence in; doubt: *Her guilty look made me suspect the truth of her excuse.* **4** person suspected: *The police have arrested two suspects in connection with the bank robbery.* 1-3 *verb,* 4 *noun.*

threat en (thret′n), **1** make a threat against; say what will be done to hurt or punish: *The teacher threatened to fail all the students that did no homework.* **2** say threats: *They threaten and scold too much.* **3** give warning of (coming trouble): *Black clouds threaten rain.* **4** be a cause of possible evil or harm to: *A flood threatened the city. verb.*

waist (wāst), **1** the part of the body between the ribs and the hips. **2** garment or part of a garment covering the body from the neck or shoulders to the hips. *noun.*

wrist (rist), the joint connecting hand and arm. *noun.*

Words in Sentences

Number from 1 to 20 on your answer sheet. Next to each numeral, write the word that belongs on that blank line in the sentence. Use the words at the left of each sentence. Use the Mini-Dictionary on the opposite page to find the meaning(s) of each word you don't know.

shove
quarrel
shoulder

During their _____1_____ , Betty Lou grabbed her brother by the _____2_____ and gave him a hard _____3_____ .

jail
freedom

People looking out from behind the barred windows of the _____4_____ wanted their _____5_____ more than anything else in the world.

accuse
nervous
suspect

I _____6_____ that Leona took the candy because she looks so _____7_____ , but I don't want to be the one to _____8_____ her.

wrist
prisoner
fist

The _____9_____ made a _____10_____ at us as he was led away, but he couldn't attack because a guard was holding on to each _____11_____ .

court
equal

In a _____12_____ of law, all people are supposed to be _____13_____ .

stolen
arrest

The bank will pay a reward for information leading to the _____13_____ of the thief or the return of the _____15_____ money, or both.

capture
surrender
prison

They trapped the man who escaped from _____16_____ and gave him a chance to _____17_____ before they moved in to _____18_____ him.

threaten
waist

When Marie's brother grabbed her around the _____19_____ , Marie had to _____20_____ to yell for help before he would let her go.

Check your answers with the key.

A

Number from 21 to 27 on your answer sheet. Next to each numeral, write the word from the box that means about the **same** as the word(s) at the right.

nervous	equal
surrender	prison
quarrel	shove
arrest	

B

Number from 28 to 35 on your answer sheet. Next to each numeral, write the word from the box that completes the story.

court	prisoner
fist	shoulder
freedom	waist
jail	wrist

C

Number your answer sheet from 36 to 40. Next to each numeral, write the word from the box that completes the sentence.

accuse	suspect
threaten	capture
stolen	

A

21. jail _____
22. stop _____
23. push hard _____
24. give up _____
25. argue _____
26. jumpy _____
27. the same _____

—— **Check your answers with the key.** ——

B

28. I'd like to be free of this terrible hole;
I'm held here by forces beyond my control.
I'm a _____ .

29. I don't come into being 'til your fingers curl up tight;
You make me when you're angry, though that's not always right.
I'm your _____ .

30. The judge calls me to order and decides right and wrong;
If you must fight to win your rights, then I'm where you belong.
I'm a _____ .

31. I join the bones inside your arm to the bones inside your hand.
When you decide to wear a watch, I'm where you place the band.
I'm your _____ .

32. They all think that they want to have me, and they want to have me now!
When they can do what they want with me, they do not always know how!
I am _____ .

33. I keep your arm from falling off. That's one thing I can do.
I make a place for your friends to lean on, but I have no room for you!
I'm your _____ .

34. I have bars on each window and locks on each door.
You won't get to know me if you know the score!
I'm a _____ .

35. I keep your legs away from your chest.
If your belt is too tight, I won't let you rest.
I'm your _____ .

—— **Check your answers with the key.** ——

C

36. fierce : gentle : : free : _____
37. fellow : man : : doubt : _____
38. give a signal : wave : : give warning : _____
39. foolish : fool : : accusing : _____
40. wear : worn : : steal : _____

—— **Check your answers with the key.** ——

54

Before you do the Words in Stories exercise, take the *Spelling Recognition Test* on page 139 and check your answers with the key at the back of the book.

A

Number from 41 to 45 on your answer sheet. Next to each numeral, write the word from the box that completes the sentence.

stolen	accuse
nervous	prison
court	

B

Number from 46 to 50 on your answer sheet. Next to each numeral, write the word from the box that completes the sentence.

quarrel	threaten
equal	shove
surrender	

C

Number from 51 to 55 on your answer sheet. Next to each numeral, write the word from the box that completes the sentence.

fist	arrest
suspect	waist
shoulder	

D

Number from 56 to 60 on your answer sheet. Next to each numeral, write the word from the box that completes the sentence.

capture	prisoner
freedom	jail
wrist	

A

When the judge called the _____41_____ to order, Brenda James wasn't worried, and when she heard the charges against her, Brenda just laughed. They would never send her to the state _____42_____ .

So she *had* been wearing five extra sweaters when she walked out of the department store! That didn't prove the goods were _____43_____ . But it did make Brenda _____44_____ to hear the store detective _____45_____ her, in front of the judge, of stealing. Who would have thought that that "customer" really worked for the store!

B

Bob Cat and Tom Cat were about the same size, and their strength was about _____46_____ . But they couldn't agree between them as to which one was stronger. Soon they started to _____47_____ . By accident, Bob Cat brushed against Tom Cat. "You'd better not _____48_____ me around!" cried Tom Cat. "I'm warning you!" Then he began to _____49_____ Bob Cat until Bob Cat showed his teeth and really started to fight. "I know I'm stronger than you are," said Tom Cat, "but I get scared more easily. Please don't bite. I _____50_____ !"

C

At the police station, they had to laugh when they talked about Slow Joe. He really was the nicest guy in the world. Once you knew Joe, you could never _____51_____ him of doing anything wrong, but he sure looked mean and evil. And Joe was big! When he curled his fingers into a _____52_____ , it looked as big as your head. Each _____53_____ was so heavy and wide, Joe looked just like a fighter. His _____54_____ was a full forty-two inches.

One day Joe went to see a movie and forgot to bring his money. When he found out his money was missing, Slow Joe grabbed a little old lady who was standing next to him in the crowd. "I want you to _____55_____ this woman," he cried. "She must have picked my pocket!"

D

In the back seat of the general's car were two captains in the People's Army. In between them sat an enemy of the state whom they had taken _____56_____ . The man's arms were tied with a thick rope that held each _____57_____ tightly together. Somehow the man threw open the door and rolled out! It seemed that he cared more for his _____58_____ than he did for his life. The captains would have to _____59_____ the man before the general found out. If they didn't, they would spend the rest of their lives in _____60_____ just like the other enemies of the state!

—— **Check your answers with the key.** ——

ac tion (ak′shən), **1** doing something: *The quick action of the firemen saved the building from being burned down.* **2** something done; act: *Giving the dog food was a kind action.* **3** way of working: *A child can push our lawn mower, because it has such an easy action.* **4** battle; part of a battle: *My uncle was wounded in action.* **5** actions, conduct or behavior: *Her actions revealed her thoughtfulness.* *noun.*

ac tor (ak′tər), person who acts on the stage, in motion pictures, on television, or over the radio. *noun.*

bul let (bùl′it), piece of lead, steel, or other metal shaped to be fired from a pistol, rifle, or other small gun. *noun.*

cast (kast), **1** throw: *cast a stone, cast a fishing line. She was cast into the water when the railing of the bridge broke.* **2** throw off; let fall; shed: *The snake cast its skin.* **3** distance a thing is thrown; throw: *The fisherman made a long cast with his line.* **4** direct or turn: *She cast a glance of surprise at me.* **5** put on record: *I cast my vote for President of the United States.* **6** shape by pouring or squeezing into a mold to harden. Metal is first melted and then cast. **7** thing shaped in a mold: *The sculptor made a cast of Queen Elizabeth.* **8** mold used to shape or support: *My cousin's broken arm is in a plaster cast.* **9** select for a part in a play: *The teacher cast me in the role of Christopher Columbus.* **10** actors in a play: *The cast was listed on the program.* **11** outward form or look; appearance: *His face had a gloomy cast.* **12** a slight amount of color; tinge: *a white shirt with a pink cast.* 1,2,4-6,9 *verb,* **cast, cast ing;** 3,7,8,10-12 *noun.*

char ac ter (kar′ik tər), **1** all the qualities or features of anything; kind; sort; nature: *The soil on the prairies is of a different character from that in the mountains.* **2** moral nature; moral strength or weakness. The special way in which you feel, think, and act, considered as good or bad, makes up your character. *She has an honest, dependable character.* **3** person or animal in a play, poem, story, or book: *My favorite character in "Charlotte's Web" is Wilbur, the pig.* **4** person who attracts attention by being different or odd: *My great-grandmother was considered a character because she smoked a corncob pipe.* **5** letter, mark, or sign used in writing or printing: *There are 52 characters in our alphabet, consisting of 26 small letters and 26 capital letters. noun.*

cot ton (kot′n), **1** soft, white fibers in a fluffy mass around the seeds of a plant, used in making fabrics or thread. **2** plant that produces these fibers. **3** thread or cloth made of cotton. **4** made of cotton: *a cotton handkerchief.* 1-3 *noun,* 4 *adjective.*

dull (dul), **1** not sharp or pointed: *It is hard to cut with a dull knife.* **2** not bright or clear: *dull eyes, a dull color, a dull day.* **3** slow in understanding; stupid: *a dull mind. A dull person often fails to get the meaning of a joke.* **4** not felt sharply: *the dull pain of a bruise.* **5** not interesting; tiresome; boring: *a dull book.* **6** not active: *The fur coat business is usually dull in summer.* **7** make or become dull: *Chopping wood dulled the blade of the ax. This cheap knife dulls easily.* 1-6 *adjective,* 7 *verb.*

fort (fôrt), a strong building or place that can be defended against an enemy. *noun.*

hon est (on′ist), **1** fair and upright; truthful; not lying, cheating, or stealing: *They are honest people.*

2 obtained by fair means; without lying, cheating, or stealing: *They made an honest profit. He lived an honest life.* **3** not hiding one's real nature; frank; open: *She has an honest face.* **4** not mixed with something of less value; genuine; pure: *Stores should sell honest goods. adjective.*

leath er (leᴛʜ′ər), **1** material made from the skins of animals by removing the hair and then tanning them: *Shoes are made of leather.* **2** made of leather: *leather gloves.* 1 *noun,* 2 *adjective.*

mag a zine (mag′ə zēn′), **1** publication appearing regularly, containing stories and articles by various writers. Most magazines are published either weekly or monthly. **2** room in a fort or warship for storing gunpowder and other dangerous substances that might explode. **3** building for storing gunpowder, guns, food, or other supplies. **4** place for cartridges in a repeating rifle or revolver. **5** place for holding a roll or reel of film in a camera or projector. *noun.*

ma ter i al (mə tir′ē əl), **1** what a thing is made from or done with: *dress material, building materials, writing materials, the material of which history is made.* **2** of matter or things; physical: *the material world.* **3** of the body: *Food and shelter are material comforts.* **4** that matters; important: *Hard work was a material factor in his success.* 1 *noun,* 2-4 *adjective.*

mov ie (mü′vē), **1** motion picture. **2 the movies,** a showing of motion pictures: *to go to the movies. noun.*

mus tache (mus′tash), **1** hair growing on a man's upper lip. **2** hairs or bristles growing near the mouth of an animal. *noun.*

pun ish (pun′ish), **1** cause pain, loss, or discomfort to for some fault or offense: *The parents punished the naughty children.* **2** cause pain, loss, or discomfort for: *The law punishes crime. verb.*

rare[1] (rer *or* rar), **1** seldom seen or found. **2** not happening often: *Snow is rare in Florida.* **3** unusually good: *Edison had rare powers as an inventor.* **4** thin; not dense: *The higher we go above the earth, the rarer the air is. adjective,* **rar er, rar est.**

rare[2] (rer *or* rar), not cooked much: *a rare steak. adjective,* **rar er, rar est.**

slen der (slen′dər), **1** long and thin; not big around; slim: *a slender child. A pencil is a slender piece of wood.* **2** slight; small: *a slender meal, a slender income, a slender hope. adjective.*

suc ceed (sək sēd′), **1** turn out well; do well; have success: *The plan succeeded.* **2** come next after; follow; take the place of: *John Adams succeeded Washington as President. Week succeeds week. verb.*

west ern (wes′tərn), **1** toward the west. **2** from the west. **3** of or in the west. **4 Western, a** of or in the western part of the United States. **b** of or in the countries in Europe or America. **5** story, motion picture, or television show about life in the western part of the United States, especially cowboy life. 1-4 *adjective,* 5 *noun.*

wig wam (wig′wom), hut of poles covered with bark, mats, or skins, made by certain North American Indians. *noun.*

Words in Sentences

Number from 1 to 20 on your answer sheet. Next to each numeral, write the word that belongs on that blank line in the sentence. Use the words at the left of each sentence. Use the Mini-Dictionary on the opposite page to find the meaning(s) of each word you don't know.

___bullet___

___movies___

___character___

In the ____1____ , a real shell is never fired when a ____2____ is supposed to be "hit" by a ____3____ from a gun.

___cotton___

___actor___

When an ____4____ does a dangerous scene, he wears a coat stuffed with ____5____ for protection.

___western___

___fort___

Did you enjoy the scene in that ____6____ where the troops defended the army ____7____ against attack?

___cast___

___slender___

___mustache___

My favorite person in the play's ____8____ was the ____9____ young man with the thick ____10____ .

___dull___

___action___

There was so little ____11____ in that book that I found it very ____12____ indeed.

___leather___

___wigwam___

In one scene they showed a ____13____ that was made of ____14____ instead of bark.

___material___

___magazine___

Did you see the picture of that dress ____15____ in the new women's ____16____ ?

___honest___

___punish___

She feels that someone will ____17____ her if she is not completely ____18____ .

___succeed___

___rare___

It is very ____19____ for one's every plan to ____20____ .

──── **Check your answers with the key.** ────

A

Number from 21 to 27 on your answer sheet. Next to each numeral, write the word from the box that means about the **opposite** of the word at the right.

dull	honest
punish	action
rare	slender
succeed	

B

Number from 28 to 35 on your answer sheet. Next to each numeral, write the word from the box that answers the question.

magazine	western
character	cast
fort	movies
cotton	mustache

C

Number from 36 to 40 on your answer sheet. Next to each numeral, write the word from the box that completes the group.

bullet	wigwam
leather	actor
material	

A

21. fail _____
22. interesting _____
23. stillness _____
24. lying _____
25. reward _____
26. fat _____
27. common _____

—— **Check your answers with the key.** ——

B

28. Who "lives" in a book or a play? _____
29. What can you defend against the enemy? _____
30. Where do you often eat popcorn in the dark? _____
31. What gives you a "stiff" upper lip? _____
32. What room in a fort holds the gunpowder and other things that explode? _____
33. What kind of story tells about cowboys and their lives? _____
34. What can you do to a rock or a play? _____
35. What kind of plant is used to make clothing? _____

—— **Check your answers with the key.** ——

C

36. clothing : cotton : : shoe : _____
37. tool : hammer : : shelter : _____
38. dress : clothing : : wool : _____
39. sail : sailor : : act : _____
40. bow : arrow : : gun : _____

—— **Check your answers with the key.** ——

Before you do the Words in Stories exercise, take the *Spelling Recognition Test* on page 140 and check your answers with the key at the back of the book.

 A

Number from 41 to 45 on your answer sheet. Next to each numeral, write the word from the box that completes the sentence.

cotton	magazine
material	succeed
leather	

B

Number from 46 to 50 on your answer sheet. Next to each numeral, write the word from the box that completes the sentence.

cast	fort
wigwam	movies
bullet	

C

Number from 51 to 55 on your answer sheet. Next to each numeral, write the word from the box that completes the sentence.

action	western
honest	punish
mustache	

D

Number from 56 to 60 on your answer sheet. Next to each numeral, write the word from the box that completes the sentence.

slender	rare
actor	character
dull	

A

In Ginger's _____41_____ there were directions and pictures that showed how to make a beautiful _____42_____ dress. The woman in the pictures was wearing a belt of red _____43_____ with the dress. The belt and the _____44_____ for the dress would not cost much at all.

Ginger decided to make the dress right away. Even though this was her first try, Ginger felt sure she would _____45_____ .

B

When people go to the _____46_____ , they usually think only about the people who appear in the picture. But there are many workers on the picture set who are not part of the _____47_____ .

Some load and shoot the cameras or control the lights; others gather information to make sure the buildings on the set look like the real thing. An Indian _____48_____ made of animal skins, or an army _____49_____ with high walls, must look true to life. Still other workers build the stage sets. They even make holes in the wall to show the mark of each "enemy _____50_____ ."

C

The Barnyard Beasts were putting on a play about the Wild West. In their _____51_____ , each of the good guys wore a black hat and a thick _____52_____ that made them look mean. The bad guys were all slow, hard-working, and very _____53_____ . The _____54_____ in the play was quite simple. The good guys were able to _____55_____ the bad guys by running them all out of town.

D

Jamey is a young _____56_____ who was chosen to play an important part in a new play that will open soon. The _____57_____ Jamey is to play on the stage is supposed to be heavy-set, but Jamey is tall and _____58_____ . To help him look the part, he ate enough food to put on twenty pounds! Then he practiced making himself as uninteresting as possible because he was supposed to play a _____59_____ person.

Finally, Jamey did something even more unusual. Even though he's gentle by nature, Jamey worked at becoming hard and mean. It's _____60_____ for someone to try that hard to fit the part.

—— **Check your answers with the key.** ——

a mount (ə mount′), **1** total sum: *What is the amount of the bill for the groceries?* **2** quantity or number (of something): *No amount of coaxing would make the dog leave its owner.* **3** reach; add up: *The loss from the flood amounts to ten million dollars.* **4** be equal: *Keeping what belongs to another amounts to stealing.* 1,2 *noun,* 3,4 *verb.*

at ten tion (ə ten′shən), **1** act or fact of attending; heed: *Pay attention to the teacher.* **2** power of attending; notice: *She called my attention to the problem.* **3** care and thought; consideration: *The children showed their grandparents much attention.* **4 attentions,** acts of courtesy or devotion: *She received many attentions, such as invitations to parties, candy, and flowers.* **5** a military attitude of readiness: *The private stood at attention during inspection. noun.*

colo nel (kėr′nl), officer who commands a regiment of soldiers. *noun.*

cot (kot), narrow bed, sometimes made of canvas stretched on a frame that folds together. *noun.*

de liv er y (di liv′ər ē), **1** carrying and giving out letters or goods: *There is one delivery of mail a day in our city.* **2** giving up; handing over: *The captive was released upon the delivery of the ransom.* **3** manner of speaking; way of giving a speech or lecture: *The speaker had an excellent delivery.* **4** act or way of striking or throwing: *That pitcher has a fast delivery.* **5** giving birth to a child. *noun, plural* **de liv er ies.**

eight een (ā′tēn′), eight more than ten; 18. *noun, adjective.*

eighth (ātth), **1** next after the seventh. **2** one of eight equal parts. *adjective, noun.*

jeep (jēp), a small but powerful automobile, used for many purposes by soldiers, farmers, and builders. *noun.* [*Jeep* probably comes from a fast way of pronouncing *G.P.,* the abbreviation for General Purpose Car. That was the name by which this type of automobile was known in the United States Army during World War II.]

meas ure (mezh′ər), **1** find the size or amount of (anything); find how long, wide, deep, large, or much (a thing) is: *We measured the room and found it was 20 feet long and 15 feet wide. We measured the pail by finding out how many quarts of water it would hold.* **2** mark off or out (in inches, feet, quarts, or some other unit): *Measure off 2 yards of this silk. Measure out a bushel of potatoes.* **3** compare with a standard or with some other person or thing by estimating, judging, or acting: *I'll measure my swimming ability with yours by racing you across the pool.* **4** be of a certain size or amount: *Buy some paper that measures 8 by 10 inches.* **5** find out size or amount: *Can she measure accurately?* **6** size or amount: *His waist measure is 30 inches.* **7** something with which to measure. A foot rule, a yardstick, and a quart dipper are common measures. **8** a unit or standard of measure, such as an inch, mile, acre, peck, quart, or gallon. **9** system of measurement: *liquid measure, dry measure, square measure.* **10** quantity, degree, or proportion: *Carelessness is in large measure responsible for many accidents.* **11** particular movement or arrangement in poetry or music: *the measure in which a poem or song is written.* **12** bar of music. **13** action meant as means to an end: *What measures shall we take to solve this problem?* **14** a proposed law; a law: *This measure has passed the Senate.* 1-5 *verb,* **meas ured, meas ur ing;** 6-14 *noun.*
measure up to, meet the standard of: *The movie did not measure up to my expectations.*

med al (med′l), piece of metal like a coin, with a figure or inscription stamped on it: *She received the gold medal for winning the race. noun.*

mo tion (mō′shən), **1** movement; moving; change of position or place. Anything is in motion which is not at rest. *Can you feel the motion of the ship?* **2** make a movement, as of the hand or head, to show one's meaning: *She motioned to show us the way.* **3** show (a person) what to do by such a motion: *He motioned me out.* **4** a formal suggestion made in a meeting, to be voted on: *I made a motion to adjourn.* 1,4 *noun,* 2,3 *verb.*

of fi cer (ô′fə sər), **1** person who commands others in the armed forces. Majors, generals, captains, and admirals are officers. **2** person who holds a public, church, or government office: *a health officer, a police officer.* **3** the president, vice-president, secretary, or treasurer of a club or society. *noun.*

po si tion (pə zish′ən), **1** place where a thing or person is: *The flowers grew in a sheltered position behind the house.* **2** way of being placed: *Put the baby in a comfortable position.* **3** proper place: *The band got into position to march in the parade.* **4** job: *He has a position in a bank.* **5** rank; standing, especially high standing: *She was raised to the position of manager.* **6** way of thinking; set of opinions: *What is your position on this question? noun.*

quart (kwôrt), **1** a unit for measuring liquids equal to one fourth of a gallon: *a quart of milk.* **2** a unit for measuring dry things equal to one eighth of a peck: *a quart of berries. noun.*

re mind (ri mīnd′), make (one) think of something; cause to remember: *This picture reminds me of a story I heard. verb.*

ri fle (rī′fəl), **1** gun with spiral grooves in its long barrel which spin or twist the bullet as it is shot. A rifle is usually fired from the shoulder. **2** search thoroughly and rob; steal. 1 *noun,* 2 *verb,* **ri fled, ri fling.**

sa lute (sə lüt′), **1** honor in a formal manner by raising the hand to the head, by firing guns, or by dipping flags: *We salute the flag every day at school. The soldier saluted the officer.* **2** meet with kind words, a bow, a kiss, or other greeting; greet: *The old gentleman walked along the avenue saluting his friends.* **3** act of saluting; sign of welcome or honor: *The queen gracefully acknowledged the salutes of the crowd.* **4** position of the hand or a gun in saluting. 1,2 *verb,* **sa lut ed, sa lut ing;** 3,4 *noun.* [*Salute* comes from a Latin word meaning "to wish good health to" or "to greet."]

sol dier (sōl′jər), **1** person who serves in an army. **2** person in the army who is not a commissioned officer. **3** person who serves in any cause: *Christian soldiers. noun.* [*Soldier* comes from a Latin word meaning "a Roman gold coin." Soldiers were called this because they served in an army for pay.]

sup ply (sə plī′), **1** furnish; provide: *The school supplies books for the children. A well supplies us with water.* **2** quantity ready for use; stock; store: *Our school gets its supplies of books, paper, pencils, and chalk from the city. We have a large supply of vegetables in the freezer.* **3 supplies,** the food and equipment necessary for an army, expedition, or the like. **4** make up for; fill: *Rocks and stumps supplied the place of chairs at the picnic.* 1,4 *verb,* **sup plied, sup ply ing;** 2,3 *noun plural* **sup plies.**

u ni form (yü′nə fôrm), **1** always the same; not changing: *The earth turns at a uniform rate.* **2** all alike; not varying: *All the bricks have a uniform size.* **3** clothes worn by the members of a group when on duty. Soldiers, policemen, and nurses wear uniforms so that they may be easily recognized. **4** clothe or furnish with a uniform. 1,2 *adjective,* 3 *noun,* 4 *verb.*

Words in Sentences

Number from 1 to 20 on your answer sheet. Next to each numeral, write the word that belongs on that blank line in the sentence. Use the words at the left of each sentence. Use the Mini-Dictionary on the opposite page to find the meaning(s) of each word you don't know.

salute

colonel

attention

The private stood at _____1_____ and gave a _____2_____ when the _____3_____ walked by.

medal

rifle

Maria received a gold _____4_____ for being the best _____5_____ shot on the team.

uniform

position

soldier

Your _____6_____ as a _____7_____ in the armed forces means that you must respect the _____8_____ you wear.

jeep

officer

motion

The bouncing _____9_____ of the army _____10_____ over the rough roads made the young _____11_____ sick to his stomach.

delivery

quart

At least one _____12_____ of oil was missing from the last _____13_____ from the store.

measure

amount

How are they able to _____14_____ the _____15_____ of gold in that ring?

remind

eighteen

supplies

I shouldn't have to _____16_____ you to divide the _____17_____ into _____18_____ equal parts, one for each of us.

eighth

cot

There is more than one _____19_____ in the room; yours is the _____20_____ one on the left.

—— **Check your answers with the key.** ——

A

Number from 21 to 26 on your answer sheet. Next to each numeral, write the word from the box that completes the sentence.

position	officer
amount	uniform
supplies	eighth

B

Number from 27 to 32 on your answer sheet. Next to each numeral, write the word from the box that completes the group.

delivery	measure
quart	eighteen
remind	motion

C

Number your answer sheet from 33 to 40. Next to each numeral, write the word from the box that completes the sentence.

cot	medal
rifle	colonel
jeep	salute
soldier	attention

A

21. Salt and flour are examples of cooking _____ .
22. A general is an example of an _____ .
23. A dozen is an example of an _____ .
24. A job at the bank is an example of a _____ .
25. Two parts of sixteen parts is an example of an _____ of the whole.
26. A policeman's set of work clothes is an example of a _____ .

—— **Check your answers with the key.** ——

B

27. stillness : rest : : movement : _____
28. discover : discovery : : deliver : _____
29. lose : point out : : forget : _____
30. seven : eight : : seventeen : _____
31. number : count : : length : _____
32. coffee : pound : : milk : _____

—— **Check your answers with the key.** ——

C

33. If you have a _____ , you should have a chest on which to pin it!
34. If you've tried a _____ , you'll enjoy a soft bed again.
35. If you're driving a _____ , you can go through rough fields.
36. If you fire a _____ , your shoulder may hurt.
37. If you wear a silver eagle on your officer's uniform, you are a _____ .
38. If you want to be a _____ , you should join the army.
39. If you like to _____ , you should be an army private.
40. If you stand at _____ , your back should be straight.

—— **Check your answers with the key.** ——

Before you do the Words in Stories exercise, take the *Spelling Recognition Test* on page 141 and check your answers with the key at the back of the book.

A

Number from 41 to 45 on your answer sheet. Next to each numeral, write the word from the box that completes the sentence.

jeep	delivery
eighth	cot
supplies	

B

Number from 46 to 50 on your answer sheet. Next to each numeral, write the word from the box that completes the sentence.

uniform	salute
attention	soldier
colonel	

C

Number from 51 to 55 on your answer sheet. Next to each numeral, write the word from the box that completes the sentence.

quart	remind
amount	measure
eighteen	

D

Number from 56 to 60 on your answer sheet. Next to each numeral, write the word from the box that completes the sentence.

position	medal
officer	rifle
motion	

A

Johnny Ace wanted to get close to nature by living in the wild. He called the camping store and then waited until the big truck stopped outside his house to make a _____41_____ . Out came a tent, a folding _____42_____ , a gas stove, and five boxes of camping _____43_____ . When Johnny had loaded the _____44_____ and final package into his new _____45_____ , he drove off into the mountains to "rough it."

B

On leave, a group of new army privates were celebrating in a big hotel. A man walked by wearing a _____46_____ covered with gold and silver thread. Every _____47_____ in the group thought the man must be a _____48_____ , or even a general! They snapped to _____49_____ and lifted their arms in a _____50_____ . "Hey, are you guys trying to be funny?" asked the doorman of the hotel.

C

The Pig Brothers decided to celebrate Karl Pig's birthday by baking a cake themselves. The directions on the package of cake mix said to use two cups of milk, but the Pig Brothers used a _____51_____ just to be sure. The next step was to add three eggs and two tablespoons of butter. But they forgot to _____52_____ the butter or count the eggs, and they used three or four times the right _____53_____ . "Please _____54_____ me to follow the directions next time," said Karl Pig. "I bet we could feed _____55_____ of us with this and still have plenty to spare!"

D

It is not enough to carry a _____56_____ ; you must know how to use it. Consuela and the other police officers practiced firing a gun once a week. From a standing _____57_____ , they tried to hit a cardboard figure that moved quickly along a wall. Instead of shooting right at the moving shape, Consuela always aimed ahead of it, in the direction of its _____58_____ . For her quick shooting and good aim, the _____59_____ in charge of Consuela's training gave her a small silver _____60_____ .

—— **Check your answers with the key.** ——

a cre (ā/kər), a unit of area equal to 160 square rods or 43,560 square feet. Land is measured in acres. *noun.*

af ford (ə fôrd/), **1** have the means; have the money, time, or strength: *Can we afford to buy a new car? He cannot afford to waste time.* **2** yield; give: *Reading this story will afford pleasure. verb.*

bush el (bùsh/əl), **1** a unit of measure for grain, fruit, vegetables, and other dry things, equal to 4 pecks or 32 quarts. **2** container that holds a bushel. *noun.*

chore (chôr), odd job; small task: *Feeding my pets is my daily chore. noun.*

crop (krop), **1** plants grown or gathered by people for their use: *Wheat, corn, and cotton are three main crops of the United States.* **2** the whole amount (of wheat, corn, or the produce of any plant or tree) which is borne in one season: *The drought made the state's potato crop very small this year.* **3** cut or bite off the top of: *Sheep had cropped the grass very short.* **4** clip or cut short: *to crop a horse's tail.* **5** act or result of cropping. A short haircut is a crop. **6** a baglike swelling of a bird's food passage. In the crop food is prepared for digestion. **7** a short whip with a loop instead of a lash. 1,2,5-7 *noun,* 3,4 *verb,* **cropped, crop ping.**

crop up, turn up unexpectedly: *All sorts of difficulties cropped up.*

ex pen sive (ek spen/siv), costly; high-priced: *He had a very expensive pen which cost $10. adjective.*

fla vor (flā/vər), **1** taste: *Chocolate and vanilla have different flavors.* **2** give added taste to; season: *We use salt, pepper, and spices to flavor food.* **3** a special quality: *Stories about ships and sailors have a flavor of the sea.* 1,3 *noun,* 2 *verb.*

fu ture (fyü/chər), **1** time to come; what is to come: *You cannot change the past, but you can do better in the future.* **2** coming; that will be: *We hope your future years will all be happy.* **3** expressing something expected to happen or exist in time to come: *the future tense of a verb.* 1 *noun,* 2,3 *adjective.*

har vest (här/vist), **1** reaping and gathering in of grain and other food crops. **2** time or season of the harvest, usually in the late summer or early autumn. **3** gather in and bring home for use: *harvest wheat.* **4** one season's yield of any natural product; crop: *The oyster harvest was small this year.* **5** result; consequences: *She is reaping the harvest of her hard work.* 1,2,4,5 *noun,* 3 *verb.*

heap (hēp), **1** pile of many things thrown or lying together: *a heap of stones, a sand heap.* **2** form into a heap; gather in heaps: *I heaped the dirty clothes beside the washing machine.* **3** a large amount: *a heap of trouble.* **4** give generously or in large amounts: *to heap praise on someone.* **5** fill full or more than full: *heap a plate with food.* 1,3 *noun,* 2,4,5 *verb.*

Oc to ber (ok tō/bər), the tenth month of the year. It has 31 days. *noun.* [*October,* the Latin name for this month, came from a Latin word meaning "eight." The month was called this because it was the eighth month in the ancient Roman calendar.]

or chard (ôr/chərd), **1** piece of ground on which fruit trees are grown. **2** the trees in an orchard: *The orchard should bear a good crop this year. noun.*

pear (per *or* par), a sweet, juicy, yellowish fruit rounded at one end and smaller toward the stem end. Pears grow on trees and are good to eat. *noun.*

quar ter (kwôr/tər), **1** one of four equal parts; half of a half; one fourth: *a quarter of an apple, a quarter of lamb. A quarter of an hour is 15 minutes.* **2** divide into fourths: *She quartered the apple.* **3** coin of the United States and Canada equal to 25 cents. Four quarters make one dollar. **4** one of four equal periods of play in certain games, such as football, basketball, or soccer. **5** one fourth of a year; 3 months: *Many savings banks pay interest every quarter.* **6** one of the four periods of the moon, lasting about 7 days each. **7** direction: *We learned that each of the four points of the compass is called a quarter. From what quarter did the wind blow?* **8** region; section; place: *The quarter where they live is near the railroad.* **9 quarters,** a place to live or stay in: *The circus has its winter quarters in the South. The servants have quarters in a cottage.* **10** give a place to live: *Soldiers were quartered in all the houses of the town.* **11** mercy shown in sparing the life of a defeated enemy: *The pirates gave no quarter to their victims.* 1,3-9,11 *noun,* 2,10 *verb.*

at close quarters, very close together; almost touching: *The cars had to pass at close quarters on the narrow mountain road.*

re spon si ble (ri spon/sə bəl), **1** obliged or expected to account for; accountable; answerable: *You are responsible for the care of your schoolbooks.* **2** deserving credit or blame: *Rain was responsible for the small attendance.* **3** trustworthy; reliable: *The class chose a responsible pupil to take care of its money.* **4** involving obligation or duties: *The President holds a very responsible position. adjective.*

scythe (sīŦH), a long, slightly curved blade on a long handle, used for mowing or reaping. *noun.*

shep herd (shep/ərd), **1** person who takes care of sheep. **2** take care of: *to shepherd a flock.* **3** guide; direct: *The teacher shepherded the children safely out of the burning building.* **4** person who cares for and protects. 1,4 *noun,* 2,3 *verb.*

sour (sour), **1** having a taste like vinegar or lemon juice; sharp and biting: *This green fruit is sour.* **2** fermented; spoiled. Sour milk is healthful, but most foods are not good to eat when they have become sour. **3** disagreeable; bad-tempered; peevish: *a sour face, a sour remark.* **4** make sour; become sour; turn sour: *The milk soured while it stood in the hot sun.* **5** make or become peevish, bad-tempered, or disagreeable. 1-3 *adjective,* 4,5 *verb.*

weed (wēd), **1** a useless or troublesome plant: *Weeds choked out the vegetables and flowers in the garden.* **2** take weeds out of: *Please weed the garden now.* 1 *noun,* 2 *verb.*

weed out, remove as useless or worthless: *I weeded out the old magazines that I no longer wanted.*

wheel bar row (hwēl/bar/ō), a small vehicle which has one wheel and two handles. A wheelbarrow holds a small load which one person can push. *noun.*

Words in Sentences

Number from 1 to 20 on your answer sheet. Next to each numeral, write the word that belongs on that blank line in the sentence. Use the words at the left of each sentence. Use the Mini-Dictionary on the opposite page to find the meaning(s) of each word you don't know.

sour

orchard

The first fruit we picked from the trees in our _____1_____ seemed _____2_____ .

pear

flavor

Which kind of summer _____3_____ do you think has the sweeter _____4_____ ?

bushel

heap

If you fill those _____5_____ baskets with that _____6_____ of fallen apples, I'll bake you some pies.

October

harvest

We expect to bring in the last of the fall _____7_____ by the end of _____8_____ .

acre

scythe

If you use a sharp _____9_____ , it takes only an hour to cut down the tall grass on an _____10_____ of land.

afford

wheelbarrow

expensive

We can't _____11_____ to buy an _____12_____ new _____13_____ right now.

quarter

future

In the _____14_____ , less than a _____15_____ of the work on a farm will be done by hand.

weed

crop

chore

To make sure we get a large _____16_____ of vegetables from the garden, give Jack the _____17_____ of pulling out each _____18_____ as it appears.

shepherd

responsible

A good _____19_____ must be _____20_____ for all of his sheep.

—— **Check your answers with the key.** ——

A

Number from 21 to 25 on your answer sheet. Next to each numeral, write the word from the box that means about the **opposite** of the word(s) at the right.

expensive	future
sour	crop
responsible	

B

Number from 26 to 33 on your answer sheet. Next to each numeral, write the word from the box that completes the group.

orchard	acre
bushel	afford
shepherd	quarter
October	pear

C

Number from 34 to 40 on your answer sheet. Next to each numeral, write the word from the box that completes the sentence.

chore	heap
flavor	harvest
wheelbarrow	scythe
weed	

A

21. careless _____

22. past _____

23. sweet _____

24. weed _____

25. costing little _____

—— **Check your answers with the key.** ——

B

26. plants : garden : : trees : _____

27. weekday : Wednesday : : month : _____

28. city : block : : farm : _____

29. meat : beef : : fruit : _____

30. children : parent : : sheep : _____

31. ten : twenty-five : : dime : _____

32. eggs : dozen : : wheat : _____

33. have a question : wonder : : have the money : _____

—— **Check your answers with the key.** ——

C

34. A _____ is a gathering in.

35. A _____ is a pile.

36. A _____ is a kind of blade.

37. A _____ is a kind of job.

38. A _____ is a kind of taste.

39. A _____ is a kind of cart.

40. A _____ is a kind of plant.

—— **Check your answers with the key.** ——

Before you do the Words in Stories exercise, take the *Spelling Recognition Test* on page 142 and check your answers with the key at the back of the book.

A

Number from 41 to 45 on your answer sheet. Next to each numeral, write the word from the box that completes the sentence.

acre	chore
weed	expensive
wheelbarrow	

B

Number from 46 to 50 on your answer sheet. Next to each numeral, write the word from the box that completes the sentence.

pear	flavor
bushel	heap
sour	

C

Number from 51 to 55 on your answer sheet. Next to each numeral, write the word from the box that completes the sentence.

October	afford
orchard	crop
harvest	

D

Number from 56 to 60 on your answer sheet. Next to each numeral, write the word from the box that completes the sentence.

scythe	quarter
shepherd	future
responsible	

A

Mrs. Hernandez had found a man who was willing to work on her vegetable farm, but the man charged a lot to do each _____41_____ . To make her farm less _____42_____ to run, Hernandez decided to do the work herself. She began by pulling up every _____43_____ in the field. After she had finished doing one _____44_____ , she had pulled up enough to fill one _____45_____ . "It's just not worth it," she said and called the man back to work for her. "He would be a good buy at twice his price!"

B

Mr. Davis was out for a Sunday drive when he saw a roadside stand that sold fresh fruit by the _____46_____ basket. Davis, who was very particular, loved nothing more than the _____47_____ of a freshly picked _____48_____ . He looked over each one in the _____49_____ of fruit piled on the table. But the more Davis looked, the less he liked what he saw. He had found only one perfect piece of fruit, and he was sure that one would taste _____50_____ !

C

By the end of _____51_____ , the last of the summer's vegetables and fruits have been picked from almost every field and _____52_____ . In ancient times, when the last _____53_____ had been gathered and stored for the winter, people felt they could _____54_____ to have a long, loud party to celebrate the _____55_____ .

D

At the New Year's party, everybody dressed up. One person came as a farmer; another, a police officer; and one even came as a _____56_____ , complete with little sheep! Lucky Duck arrived at a _____57_____ to midnight, dressed as Father Time. She had found a long, white beard and a white robe to wear, and she carried a long, shiny _____58_____ . As old Father Time, Lucky was supposed to stand for the year that had just ended. One of her friends, dressed up like a little baby, stood for the _____59_____ —the new year about to begin. At exactly midnight, Lucky told her friend, "Now my year has ended, and my job is done. During the coming year, they'll hold you _____60_____ for everything that happens!"

—— **Check your answers with the key.** ——

Review Lesson

Choose the word from each pair that best completes the sentence.

A

1. eighteen	2. flavor
3. buck	4. remind
5. succeed	6. saddle
7. buckle	8. steady
9. October	10. position
11. harvest	12. wrist
13. pants	14. slender
15. mustache	16. medal
17. leather	18. sleeve
19. acre	20. waist
21. material	22. western
23. shoulder	24. quarter
25. character	26. attention
27. movies	28. magazine
29. afford	30. threaten
31. equal	32. expensive
33. quarrel	34. future

B

35. uniform	36. soldier
37. prisoner	38. colonel
39. suspect	40. nervous
41. officer	42. shepherd
43. fort	44. prison
45. scythe	46. fist
47. freedom	48. jail
49. cast	50. eighth
51. salute	52. supplies
53. jeep	54. orchard
55. pear	56. rifle
57. tame	58. stolen
59. capture	60. measure
61. motion	62. wheelbarrow
63. weed	64. bullet
65. rare	66. rough
67. surrender	68. shove

A

On her last birthday, Donna turned ____1 or 2____ . "You're not getting any younger," her mother said.

"Please don't ____3 or 4____ me!" Donna replied. She was afraid she'd never ____5 or 6____ in finding a young man she wanted as a ____7 or 8____ date because she lived in a very small town that had few young, single men.

But on ____9 or 10____ ninth, Donna went with a girl friend to the yearly ____11 or 12____ dance which was held at the town hall. That's where Donna met Pete Porter. Pete was a tall, ____13 or 14____ cowboy with a dark ____15 or 16____ . He even wore handmade ____17 or 18____ cowboy boots to complete the picture.

When they stepped out onto the dance floor, Pete put his arm around Donna's ____19 or 20____ and spun her around the room to the beat of the country and ____21 or 22____ music. Later, when the music was slow and soft, Donna closed her eyes and leaned her head on Pete's ____23 or 24____ . There were quite a few women at the dance, but for the rest of the evening Pete didn't pay ____25 or 26____ to anyone but Donna.

The next night, Pete invited Donna to the ____27 or 28____ . On the way home he said, "Let's have dinner out as soon as I can ____29 or 30____ to give us a night on the town. We'll go to one of those ____31 or 32____ places in the city." Donna was delighted. She began to think that she and Pete just might have a wonderful ____33 or 34____ together.

B

During the last war, a ____35 or 36____ named Lou Ferris was taken ____37 or 38____ by the enemy. Although Lou was a thin, ____39 or 40____ little man, no one was able to make him give away his country's secrets. The commanding ____41 or 42____ of the ____43 or 44____ camp had Lou beaten and given extra work, but Lou just shook his ____45 or 46____ at his enemies and went on planning his escape to ____47 or 48____ .

Lou never gave up trying to escape. He finally made it on his ____49 or 50____ try. He knocked out the driver of the commander's car and drove it out through the open gates of the camp while the guards were busy unloading ____51 or 52____ . The guards immediately gave chase in a ____53 or 54____ containing the driver and one man with a high-powered ____55 or 56____ . Lou drove the ____57 or 58____ car off the road and across the fields until he saw the bank of a river just ahead. Lou decided that they would never ____59 or 60____ him alive again. He jumped from the car while it was still in ____61 or 62____ and fired a ____63 or 64____ into the gas tank. The enemy arrived just as the car hit the water and exploded. The enemy never learned if the ____65 or 66____ waters of the river were strong enough to make Lou ____67 or 68____ for the last time.

Review Lesson

C

69. rodeo	70. stable
71. hitch	72. corral
73. gallop	74. delivery
75. actor	76. stallion
77. dull	78. cotton
79. honest	80. difficult
81. weary	82. human
83. accuse	84. insist
85. crop	86. amount
87. mare	88. disgrace
89. punish	90. arrest
91. court	92. wigwam
93. quart	94. heap
95. bushel	96. cot
97. chore	98. action
99. responsible	100. sour

C

Each morning before daylight they would open the doors of the ____69 or 70____ and ____71 or 72____ the horses to the wagons loaded with the milk cans, or ice, or fresh vegetables, awaiting ____73 or 74____ . Among the horses there was one old ____75 or 76____ with a ____77 or 78____ look in his eyes, who found the daily job of pulling a heavy wagon more and more ____79 or 80____ . Even when he felt too ____81 or 82____ to pull the wagon on a level road, his driver would ____83 or 84____ that he move the cart rapidly up the hills. And when the horse just couldn't start the heavy wagon moving, the driver would beat him soundly with a thin riding ____85 or 86____ .

"That's a ____87 or 88____ !" someone would shout. "You have no right to ____89 or 90____ that poor beast simply because he has grown old. I ought to take you to ____91 or 92____ !" But in those days the people only had horses to bring to market each ____93 or 94____ of milk and each ____95 or 96____ of fruit or vegetables they were selling. Sad to say, at that time there was no department to guard the well-being of animals. And none of the people took any ____97 or 98____ because no one felt that he or she was really ____99 or 100____ .

—— **Check your answers with the key.** ——

69

an chor (ang′kər), **1** a heavy piece of iron or steel fastened to a chain or rope and dropped from a ship to the bottom of the water to hold the ship in place: *The anchor caught in the mud at the bottom of the lake and kept the boat from drifting.* **2** hold in place with an anchor: *Can you anchor the boat in this storm?* **3** stop or stay in place by using an anchor: *The ship anchored in the bay.* **4** hold in place; fix firmly: *The scouts anchored the tent to the ground.* **5** something that makes a person feel safe and secure: *The weekly talks with an understanding teacher were an anchor to the troubled child.* 1,5 *noun*, 2-4 *verb*.

aye or **ay** (ī), **1** yes: *Aye, aye, sir.* **2** an affirmative answer, vote, or voter: *The ayes won when the vote was taken.* 1 *adverb*, 2 *noun*.

bare (ber *or* bar), **1** without covering; not clothed; naked: *The sun burned his bare shoulders. The top of the hill was bare, but trees grew part way up its slope.* **2** empty; not furnished: *a room bare of furniture.* **3** plain; not adorned: *a bare little cabin in the woods.* **4** just enough and no more: *She earns only a bare living.* **5** make bare; uncover; reveal: *to bare one's feelings.* 1-4 *adjective*, **bar er, bar est;** 5 *verb*, **bared, bar ing.**

car go (kär′gō), load of goods carried by a ship or plane: *The freighter had docked to unload a cargo of wheat.* *noun*, *plural* **car goes** or **car gos.**

crew (krü), **1** the sailors needed to do the work on a ship, or to row a boat. **2** group of persons working aboard an aircraft. **3** any group of people working or acting together: *A train crew runs a railroad train.* **4** gang; mob: *The kids in that neighborhood are a rough crew.* *noun*.

east ern (ē′stərn), **1** toward the east: *an eastern trip.* **2** from the east: *eastern tourists.* **3** of the east; in the east: *eastern schools.* **4 Eastern, a** of or in the eastern part of the United States. **b** of or in the countries in Asia. *adjective*.

land lord (land′lôrd′), **1** man who owns buildings or lands that he rents to others. **2** person who runs an inn or boarding house. *noun*.

mast (mast), **1** a long pole of wood or steel set upright on a ship to support the sails and rigging. **2** any tall, upright pole: *the mast of a derrick.* *noun*. **before the mast,** serving as a common sailor, because such sailors used to sleep in the forward part of the ship.

na vy (nā′vē), a large, organized group of officers and sailors trained and equipped for war, and the ships of war on which they serve. *noun*, *plural* **na vies.**

neigh bor hood (nā′bər hùd), **1** region near some place or thing: *She lives in the neighborhood of the mill.* **2** place; district: *Is North Street in a good neighborhood?* **3** people living near one another; people of a place: *The whole neighborhood came to the big party.* **4** of a neighborhood: *a neighborhood newspaper.* 1-3 *noun*, 4 *adjective*. **in the neighborhood of,** somewhere near; about: *The car cost in the neighborhood of $3500.*

oar (ôr), **1** a long pole with a broad, flat end, used in rowing. Sometimes an oar is used to steer a boat. **2** person who rows: *He is the best oar in the crew.* *noun*.

pi rate (pī′rit), **1** person who attacks and robs ships; robber on the sea. **2** be a pirate; plunder; rob. 1 *noun*, 2 *verb*, **pi rat ed, pi rat ing.**

roy al (roi′əl), **1** of kings and queens: *the royal family.* **2** belonging to a king or queen: *royal power, a royal palace.* **3** from or by a king or queen: *a royal command.* **4** of a kingdom: *a royal army or navy.* **5** suitable for a king or queen; splendid: *a royal welcome, a royal feast.* **6** like a king or queen; noble; majestic: *The lion is a royal beast.* *adjective*.

sea port (sē′pôrt′), port or harbor on the seacoast; city or town with a harbor that ships can reach from the sea: *San Francisco is a seaport.* *noun*.

shal low (shal′ō), **1** not deep: *shallow water, a shallow dish, a shallow mind.* **2 shallows,** a shallow place: *The children splashed in the shallows of the pond.* 1 *adjective*, 2 *noun*.

stern[1] (stėrn), **1** severe; strict; harsh: *Our teacher's stern frown silenced us.* **2** hard; not yielding; firm: *stern necessity. adjective.*

stern[2] (stėrn), the rear part of a ship, boat, or aircraft. *noun*.

suit case (süt′kās′), a flat traveling bag. *noun*.

tide (tīd), **1** the rise and fall of the ocean about every twelve hours, caused by the pull of the moon and the sun. **2** anything that rises and falls like the tide: *the tide of public opinion.* **3 tide over,** help along for a time: *His savings will tide him over his illness.* 1,2 *noun*, 3 *verb*, **tid ed, tid ing.**

voy age (voi′ij), **1** a journey or travel by water; cruise: *We had a pleasant voyage to England.* **2** a journey or travel through the air or through space: *an airplane voyage, the earth's voyage around the sun.* **3** make or take a voyage; go by sea or air: *We voyaged across the Atlantic Ocean.* 1,2 *noun*, 3 *verb*, **voy aged, voy ag ing.**

wharf (hwôrf), platform built on the shore or out from the shore, beside which ships can load and unload. *noun*, *plural* **wharves** (hwôrvz) or **wharfs.**

Words in Sentences

Number from 1 to 20 on your answer sheet. Next to each numeral, write the word that belongs on that blank line in the sentence. Use the words at the left of each sentence. Use the Mini-Dictionary on the opposite page to find the meaning(s) of each word you don't know.

seaport	From my house in the old _____1_____ , I could see
wharf	the ships pulling in to the _____2_____ of the busy
neighborhood	_____3_____ .

suitcase	The _____4_____ said he had given the room to a
landlord	sailor carrying a small leather _____5_____ .

pirate	Years ago, a ship carrying a _____6_____ of gold and
voyage	silver on an ocean _____7_____ had to be on guard
cargo	against _____8_____ ships.

eastern	The king and the others in the _____9_____ family left
royal	the castle through the _____10_____ gate to examine
navy	the new ships in the _____11_____ .

crew	Long ago a ship captain could punish any sailor in his
bare	_____12_____ by having the man tied to the
mast	_____13_____ of the ship and whipped across his
	_____14_____ back.

shallow	When the _____15_____ is low, you have to use an
tide	_____16_____ to push the boat out of the
oar	_____17_____ water.

Aye	Any good sailor says " _____18_____ , sir," when the
stern	captain orders the _____19_____ raised and pulled in
anchor	over the ship's _____20_____ .

—— **Check your answers with the key.** ——

A

Number from 21 to 26 on your answer sheet. Next to each numeral, write the word from the box that means about the **opposite** of the word at the right.

shallow	royal
bare	stern
aye	eastern

B

Number from 27 to 30 on your answer sheet. Next to each numeral, write the word that can be made by adding one word from the box to the word at the right.

case	hood
sea	land

C

Number from 31 to 40 on your answer sheet. Next to each numeral, write the word from the box that completes the sentence.

pirate	anchor
oar	tide
mast	cargo
crew	navy
wharf	voyage

A

21. no   _____
22. western   _____
23. gentle   _____
24. covered   _____
25. common   _____
26. deep   _____

—— **Check your answers with the key.** ——

B

27. under : understand : : neighbor : _____
28. water : glass : : clothes : _____
29. car : garage : : ship : _____
30. sheep : shepherd : : apartment : _____

—— **Check your answers with the key.** ——

C

31. I work on board an airplane.
    I'm one of the _____ .

32. I'm a sailor trained for war.
    I'm part of the _____ .

33. I hold in place.
    I'm an _____ .

34. I rise and fall when the moon moves me.
    I'm the _____ .

35. They row with two of me.
    I'm an _____ .

36. I keep the sails high in the air.
    I'm the _____ .

37. I'm loaded and unloaded.
    I'm a _____ .

38. I'm a sea-going thief.
    I'm a _____ .

39. I'm a kind of trip.
    I'm a _____ .

40. I am where they load and unload.
    I'm a _____ .

—— **Check your answers with the key.** ——

Before you do the Words in Stories exercise, take the *Spelling Recognition Test* on page 143 and check your answers with the key at the back of the book.

Number from 41 to 45 on your answer sheet. Next to each numeral, write the word from the box that completes the sentence.

stern	anchor
voyage	eastern
tide	

Number from 46 to 50 on your answer sheet. Next to each numeral, write the word from the box that completes the sentence.

mast	royal
navy	Aye
pirate	

Number from 51 to 55 on your answer sheet. Next to each numeral, write the word from the box that completes the sentence.

shallow	wharf
oar	suitcase
bare	

Number from 56 to 60 on your answer sheet. Next to each numeral, write the word from the box that completes the sentence.

landlord	cargo
neighborhood	seaport
crew	

A

The sun was rising and the _____41_____ sky was just becoming light. Little by little, the ocean waves covered the wide, sandy beach; the _____42_____ was rising too. Out in deep water, the men were raising the ship's _____43_____ from the ocean floor. When they had pulled it in over the ship's _____44_____, everything would be ready. The _____45_____ could then begin.

B

Captain Jamison commands one of the fighting ships in the king's _____46_____. Today the king's brother is on board, along with several others in the _____47_____ family.

Jamison is worried. He had sent a man up to the top of the tall _____48_____ that holds the main sails of the ship and told him to act as look-out. "_____49_____, Captain," the man answered. Less than an hour later he had reported what Jamison most feared to hear. A ship, carrying heavy guns and flying a black flag, was drawing near. It was a _____50_____ ship!

C

It had been a frightening trip over hundreds of miles of ocean for Poonti. The boat was small, much too small for the 120 people on board. A war was tearing apart Poonti's nation, which is why he and all the other people on the boat left their country in the middle of the night without so much as a _____51_____ of clothing between them. They hoped to reach Florida in a few days' time, but it was not to be.

After two days at sea, they ran into a storm. The boat turned over, and Poonti found himself in the ocean. He grabbed onto an _____52_____ floating by and used it to right himself in the ocean as the waves tossed him about. Poonti was used to swimming in much more calm and _____53_____ water, but at least he was a strong swimmer.

Poonti was luckier than most of the others who had been on the boat. He was one of only twenty that a passing ship picked up. The rest, the ocean took. Having done the best he could, the rescue ship's captain sailed to the nearest island. Poonti had not made it as far as America after all. Still, as he walked off the ship, the wood of the _____54_____ felt good under his _____55_____ feet. As long as he was alive, there was hope. One day Poonti would make it to America. He was sure of it.

D

In the days when sailing ships were common, the largest cities were along the coast. When a ship arrived at such a _____56_____, the ship's _____57_____ would be unloaded at once. Then the _____58_____ would head for a _____59_____ where there were rows and rows of inns. And when the ship was ready to sail again, the only person left in each house would be the _____60_____.

Check your answers with the key.

awk ward (ôk′wərd), **1** clumsy; not graceful or skillful in movement: *Seals are very awkward on land, but graceful in the water.* **2** not well suited to use: *The handle of this pitcher has an awkward shape.* **3** not easily managed: *This is an awkward corner to turn.* **4** embarrassing: *He asked me such an awkward question that I did not know what to reply. adjective.*

bliz zard (bliz′ərd), a blinding snowstorm with a very strong wind and very great cold. *noun.*

blub ber (blub′ər), **1** fat of whales and some other sea animals. Oil obtained from whale blubber was burned in lamps. **2** weep noisily. 1 *noun,* 2 *verb.*

Es ki mo (es′kə mō), **1** member of a people living in the arctic regions of North America and northeastern Asia. **2** language of the Eskimos. **3** of or having to do with the Eskimos or their language. 1,2 *noun, plural* **Es ki mos** or **Es ki mo** for 1; 3 *adjective.*

fur nace (fėr′nis), an enclosed chamber or box to make a very hot fire in. Furnaces are used to heat buildings, melt metals, and make glass. *noun.*

glow (glō), **1** shine because of heat; be red-hot or white-hot: *Embers still glowed in the fireplace after the fire had died down.* **2** the shine from something that is red-hot or white-hot: *the glow of molten steel.* **3** a similar shine without heat: *the glow of gold.* **4** give off light without heat: *Some clocks glow in the dark.* **5** a bright, warm color: *the glow of sunset.* **6** the warm feeling or color of the body: *the glow of health on her cheeks.* **7** show a warm color; look warm: *His cheeks glowed as he jogged.* **8** an eager look on the face: *a glow of excitement.* **9** look eager: *Their eyes glowed at the thought of a trip.* 1,4,7,9 *verb,* 2,3,5,6,8 *noun.*

grad u al (graj′ü əl), by degrees too small to be separately noticed; little by little: *This low hill has a gradual slope. adjective,* **gradually,** *adverb.*

hun ger (hung′gər), **1** pains in the stomach caused by having had nothing to eat. **2** desire or need for food: *I ate an apple to satisfy my hunger.* **3** feel hunger; be hungry. **4** strong desire: *The bright boy had a hunger for knowledge.* **5** have a strong desire: *to hunger for affection, to hunger for friends.* 1,2,4 *noun,* 3,5 *verb.*

i cy (ī′sē), **1** like ice; very cold: *icy fingers.* **2** covered with ice; slippery: *The car skidded on the icy street.* **3** of ice: *an icy snowball.* **4** without warm feeling; cold and unfriendly: *She gave me an icy stare. adjective,* **i ci er, i ci est.**

kay ak (kī′ak), an Eskimo canoe made of skins stretched over a light frame of wood or bone with an opening in the middle for a person. *noun.*

north ern (nôr′ᴛнərn), **1** toward the north: *the northern side of a building.* **2** coming from the north: *a northern breeze.* **3** of or in the north: *They have traveled in northern countries.* **4** **Northern,** of or in the northern part of the United States: *Boston is a Northern city. adjective.*

pad dle (pad′l), **1** a short oar with a broad blade at one end or both ends, usually held with both hands in rowing a boat or canoe. **2** move (a boat or a canoe) with a paddle or paddles. **3** act of paddling; a turn at the paddle. **4** one of the broad boards fixed around a water wheel or a paddle wheel to push, or be pushed by, the water. **5** a broad piece of wood with a handle at one end, used for stirring, for mixing, for beating clothes, and in other ways. **6** beat with a paddle; spank. 1,3-5 *noun,* 2,6 *verb,* **pad dled, pad dling.**

po lar (pō′lər), of or near the North or South Pole: *It is very cold in the polar regions. adjective.*

re frig e ra tor (ri frij′ə rā′tər), something that keeps things cool. An electric refrigerator keeps food cool without ice. *noun.*

rein deer (rān′dir′), a large deer with branching antlers that lives in northern regions. It is used to pull sleighs and also for meat, milk, and hides. *noun, plural* **rein deer.**

seal[1] (sēl), **1** design stamped on a piece of wax or other soft material, used to show ownership or authority. The seal of the United States is attached to important government papers. **2** stamp for marking things with such a design: *a seal with one's initials on it.* **3** piece of wax, paper, or metal on which the design is stamped. **4** mark with a seal: *The treaty was signed and sealed by both governments.* **5** close very tightly; fasten: *Seal the letter before mailing it. I sealed the jars of fruit. Her promise sealed her lips.* **6** settle; determine: *The judge's words sealed the prisoner's fate.* **7** give a sign that (a thing) is true: *They sealed their bargain by shaking hands.* **8** a special kind of stamp: *Christmas seals.* 1-3,8 *noun,* 4-7 *verb.*

seal[2] (sēl), **1** a sea animal with large flippers, usually living in cold regions. Some kinds have very valuable fur. **2** its fur. **3** leather made from the skin of a seal. *noun, plural* **seals** or **seal.**

sur round (sə round′), shut in on all sides; be around; extend around: *A high fence surrounds the field. They surrounded their children with love. verb.*

tem per a ture (tem′pər ə chər), **1** degree of heat or cold. The temperature of freezing water is 32 degrees Fahrenheit, or 0 degrees Celsius. **2** a body temperature higher than normal (98.6 degrees Fahrenheit, or 37 degrees Celsius): *A sick person may have a temperature. noun.*

wal rus (wôl′rəs), a large sea animal of the arctic regions, resembling a seal but having long tusks. Walruses are hunted for their hides, ivory tusks, and blubber oil. *noun, plural* **wal rus es** or **wal rus.** [*Walrus* comes from Dutch words meaning "whale" and "horse."]

zone (zōn), **1** any of the five great divisions of the earth's surface, bounded by imaginary lines going around the earth parallel to the equator. **2** any region or area especially considered or set off. A combat zone is a district where fighting is going on. **3** area or district in a city or town under special restrictions as to building. **4** divide into zones: *The city was zoned for factories and residences.* 1-3 *noun,* 4 *verb,* **zoned, zon ing.**

Words in Sentences

A

Number from 1 to 20 on your answer sheet. Next to each numeral, write the word that belongs on that blank line in the sentence. Use the words at the left of each sentence. Use the Mini-Dictionary on the opposite page to find the meaning(s) of each word you don't know.

Eskimo

northern

reindeer

When hunting the _____1_____ , an _____2_____ will travel for days across the cold, _____3_____ countryside.

polar

seal

The _____4_____ is prized by humans for its soft thick fur, but the _____5_____ bear hunts it for food.

blubber

walrus

icy

The _____6_____ is protected against the cold of the _____7_____ waters by its thick fur and the _____8_____ under its skin.

temperature

refrigerator

The _____9_____ inside a _____10_____ is supposed to remain cold.

furnace

glow

There was a bright, cheerful _____11_____ coming from the open door of the coal _____12_____ .

hunger

awkward

zone

Weak from _____13_____ and holding his rifle in an _____14_____ position, the soldier moved dangerously close to the enemy's _____15_____ .

gradually

blizzard

The winter season's worst _____16_____ first struck the large town on the hill, then _____17_____ moved on down the valley.

kayak

surround

paddle

An Eskimo must be able to _____18_____ a _____19_____ swiftly through the icy waters that _____20_____ the village.

—— **Check your answers with the key.** ——

A

Number from 21 to 28 on your answer sheet. Next to each numeral, write the word from the box that means about the **same** as the word(s) at the right.

blubber	zone
gradually	awkward
seal	paddle
surround	glow

B

Number from 29 to 34 on your answer sheet. Next to each numeral, write the word from the box that completes the sentence.

kayak	blizzard
reindeer	refrigerator
temperature	walrus

C

Number from 35 to 40 on your answer sheet. Next to each numeral, write the word from the box that completes the group.

polar	icy
northern	Eskimo
hunger	furnace

A

21. put around _____
22. area _____
23. shine softly _____
24. hard to handle _____
25. little by little _____
26. hit _____
27. fat _____
28. stamp _____

—— **Check your answers with the key.** ——

B

29. They want my milk and meat.
    I'm a _____ .

30. I go from high to low.
    I'm a _____ .

31. I keep blowing and freezing.
    I'm a _____ .

32. They want my teeth and fat.
    I'm a _____ .

33. They can make me from animal skin and bones.
    I'm a _____ .

34. I keep things cool.
    I'm a _____ .

—— **Check your answers with the key.** ——

C

35. rock : rocky : : ice : _____
36. canoe : Indian : : kayak : _____
37. cold : hot : : refrigerator : _____
38. north : northern : : pole : _____
39. medicine : disease : : food : _____
40. east : north : : eastern : _____

—— **Check your answers with the key.** ——

Before you do the Words in Stories exercise, take the *Spelling Recognition Test* on page 144 and check your answers with the key at the back of the book.

A

Number from 41 to 45 on your answer sheet. Next to each numeral, write the word from the box that completes the sentence.

hunger	walrus
blubber	reindeer
Eskimo	

B

Number from 46 to 50 on your answer sheet. Next to each numeral, write the word from the box that completes the sentence.

polar	kayak
awkward	icy
paddle	

C

Number from 51 to 55 on your answer sheet. Next to each numeral, write the word from the box that completes the sentence.

furnace	refrigerator
temperature	glow
Northern	

D

Number from 56 to 60 on your answer sheet. Next to each numeral, write the word from the box that completes the sentence.

zone	seal
gradually	blizzard
surround	

A

In order to get food for their families, bands of _____41_____ in the cold North search for the animals from which they get meat. The hunters might have to track a herd of _____42_____ over the ice and snow for days before they are able to make a kill. Using great strength, they might even bring down a huge _____43_____ in order to get the life-giving _____44_____ just under its fur. Their hunting cannot always succeed, and _____45_____ is a fact of life with them.

B

In the frozen Northlands, water-loving animals often seem slow and _____46_____ on dry land. The great white _____47_____ bear is a good example. It cannot move too quickly over the piles of snow and ice, but when it swims in the _____48_____ waters of the North, it is one of the fastest hunters alive.

A man in a _____49_____ is another example of speed and know-how in the water. Using a wooden _____50_____ to move the boat through the water, he is as quick as any creature of the wild.

C

The sky began to _____51_____ with shifting colored lights. "Those are the _____52_____ Lights," said Wee Willie Whale to the traveling salesman. "Aren't they great?"

"But they're all light and no heat," replied the salesman. "What you need is something to raise the _____53_____ around here. Buy this new _____54_____ from me. It's only two dollars down with a lifetime to pay the rest."

"I'd like to buy that fire box of yours," said Willie, "but I can't afford to. I paid out all my money yesterday to a man who gave me a special deal on a new _____55_____ !"

D

For a baby _____56_____ , the safest place to be is in the middle of the strong winds and blinding snow of a _____57_____ . No hunters can attack there.

When the sun shines, though, the area of land between the nest and the water becomes a danger _____58_____ . Large groups of men rush across the ice and _____59_____ the young creatures. One by one the animals are clubbed to death so that humans may wear their fur. So many of these animals have been killed that they are _____60_____ beginning to disappear.

— **Check your answers with the key.** —

an ger (ang′gər), **1** the feeling that one has toward someone or something that hurts, opposes, offends, or annoys: *In a moment of anger, I hit my friend.* **2** make angry: *The girl's disobedience angered her parents.* 1 *noun,* 2 *verb.*

bam boo (bam bü′), a woody or treelike grass with a very tall, stiff, hollow stem that has hard, thick joints. Bamboo grows in warm regions. Its stems are used for making canes, fishing poles, furniture, and even houses. *noun,*
plural **bam boos.**

bat tle (bat′l), **1** a fight between armies, air forces, or navies: *The battle for the island lasted six months.* **2** fighting or warfare: *The soldier received his wounds in battle.* **3** any fight or contest: *The candidates fought a battle of words during the campaign.* **4** take part in a battle; fight; struggle: *battle with wolves. The swimmer had to battle a strong current.* 1-3 *noun,* 4 *verb,* **bat tled, bat tling.**

com pan ion (kəm pan′yən), **1** one who often goes along with or accompanies another; one who shares in what another is doing. **2** anything that matches or goes with another in kind, size, and color: *I can't find the companion to this shoe. noun.* [*Companion* comes from a Latin word meaning "one who eats bread with another."]

dig ni ty (dig′nə tē), **1** proud and self-respecting character or manner; stately appearance: *the dignity of a cathedral.* **2** quality of character or ability that wins the respect and high opinion of others: *A judge should maintain the dignity of his or her position.* **3** high office, rank, or title; position of honor: *the dignity of the presidency.* **4** worth; nobleness: *Honest work has dignity. n., pl.* **dig ni ties.**

e qua tor (i kwā′tər), an imaginary circle around the middle of the earth, halfway between the North Pole and the South Pole. The United States is north of the equator; Australia is south of it. *noun.*

friend ship (frend′ship), **1** condition of being friends. **2** liking between friends. **3** friendly feeling or behavior; friendliness. *noun.*

guest (gest), **1** person who is received and entertained at another's house or table; visitor. **2** person who is staying at a hotel or motel. *noun.*

hur ri cane (hėr′ə kān), storm with violent wind and, usually, very heavy rain. The wind in a hurricane blows at more than 75 miles per hour. *noun.*

hut (hut), a small, roughly made cabin: *The children built a hut in the woods. noun.*

jun gle (jung′gəl), wild land thickly overgrown with bushes, vines, and trees. Jungles are hot and humid regions with many kinds of plants and wild animals. *noun.*

league[1] (lēg), **1** union of persons, parties, or nations formed to help one another. **2** unite in a league; form a union. **3** association of sports clubs or teams: *a baseball league.* 1,3 *noun,* 2 *verb,* **leagued, lea guing.**

league[2] (lēg), an old unit for measuring length or distance, usually about 3 miles. *noun.*

south ern (su⊤H′ərn), **1** toward the south: *the southern side of a building.* **2** from the south: *a southern breeze.* **3** of or in the south: *They have traveled in southern countries.* **4 Southern,** of or in the southern part of the United States: *a Southern city. adjective.*

spear (spir), **1** weapon with a long shaft and a sharp-pointed head. **2** pierce with a spear: *The Indian speared a fish.* **3** pierce or stab with anything sharp: *spear string beans with a fork.* 1 *noun,* 2,3 *verb.*

stalk[1] (stôk), **1** the main stem of a plant. **2** any slender, supporting part of a plant or animal. A flower may have a stalk. The eyes of a lobster are on stalks. *noun.*

stalk[2] (stôk), **1** approach or pursue without being seen or heard: *The hungry lion stalked a zebra.* **2** spread silently and steadily: *Disease stalked through the land.* **3** walk in a slow, stiff, or proud manner: *She stalked into the room and threw herself into a chair.* **4** stalking. 1-3 *verb,* 4 *noun.*

swamp (swomp), **1** wet, soft land: *We will drain the swamp on our farm so that we can plant crops there.* **2** plunge or sink in a swamp or in water: *The horses were swamped in the stream.* **3** fill with water and sink: *The waves swamped the boat.* **4** overwhelm or be overwhelmed as by a flood; make or become helpless: *to be swamped with homework.* 1 *noun,* 2-4 *verb.*

ti ger (tī′gər), a large, fierce animal of Asia that has dull-yellow fur striped with black. *noun.*

trea ty (trē′tē), a formal agreement, especially one between nations, signed and approved by each nation. *noun, plural* **trea ties.**

trop i cal (trop′ə kəl), of the tropics: *Bananas are tropical fruit. adjective.*

war ri or (wôr′ē ər), a person experienced in fighting battles. *noun.*

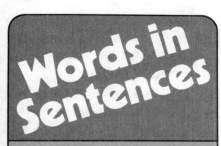

treaty

battle

league

The _____1_____ of states has now signed a _____2_____ promising never to do _____3_____ with one another again.

tropical

warrior

spear

The _____4_____ carried his _____5_____ with the point up as he walked through the _____6_____ forest.

companion

friendship

swamp

I offered to be his _____7_____ on the difficult journey through the _____8_____ , but only because of our long _____9_____ .

hut

bamboo

jungle

The little _____10_____ at the edge of the _____11_____ was made of _____12_____ poles tied together.

stalk

tiger

The _____13_____ was unable to _____14_____ the deer after the big buck's trail disappeared into the shallow waters of the river.

anger

dignity

guest

The chief of the village was angry at the way his _____15_____ had acted, but he would not lose his _____16_____ by showing any feelings of _____17_____ .

equator

hurricane

southern

A _____18_____ forms over the waters of the _____19_____ oceans just below the _____20_____ .

—— **Check your answers with the key.** ——

Number from 21 to 27 on your answer sheet. Next to each numeral, write the word from the box that completes the sentence.

anger	tiger
jungle	hut
hurricane	bamboo
league	

B

Number from 28 to 33 on your answer sheet. Next to each numeral, write the word from the box that completes the group.

equator	friendship
tropical	southern
battle	swamp

C

Number from 34 to 40 on your answer sheet. Next to each numeral, write the word from the box that completes the sentence.

stalk	guest
companion	treaty
warrior	spear
dignity	

A

21. The material called _____ is a kind of plant.
22. What we call _____ is a kind of feeling.
23. The building called a _____ is a kind of house.
24. The place we call a _____ is a kind of forest.
25. The animal called a _____ is a kind of large cat.
26. What we call a _____ is a kind of storm.
27. What we call a _____ is a kind of group.

—— **Check your answers with the key.** ——

B

28. east : eastern : : south : _____
29. dry : wet : : desert : _____
30. cold : polar : : heat : _____
31. top : North Pole : : middle : _____
32. enemy : anger : : friend : _____
33. jump : leap : : fight : _____

—— **Check your answers with the key.** ——

C

34. A _____ is thrown through the air.
35. A _____ comes to visit.
36. A _____ goes to war.
37. A _____ keeps you company.
38. A _____ shows what nations agree on.
39. A _____ supports a flower.
40. She received the medal with great _____.

—— **Check your answers with the key.** ——

Before you do the Words in Stories exercise, take the *Spelling Recognition Test* on page 145 and check your answers with the key at the back of the book.

A

Number from 41 to 45 on your answer sheet. Next to each numeral, write the word from the box that completes the sentence.

battle	dignity
warrior	treaty
league	

B

Number from 46 to 50 on your answer sheet. Next to each numeral, write the word from the box that completes the sentence.

southern	equator
hurricane	bamboo
tropical	

C

Number from 51 to 55 on your answer sheet. Next to each numeral, write the word from the box that completes the sentence.

friendship	anger
companion	guest
swamp	

D

Number from 56 to 60 on your answer sheet. Next to each numeral, write the word from the box that completes the sentence.

spear	tiger
hut	jungle
stalk	

A

The last _____41_____ between the forces of the two enemy villages cost the lives of so many men, the people decided to end the war. They signed a _____42_____ which let them live in peace together. Then each fallen _____43_____ was carried off the field and laid to rest with honor and _____44_____.

Later, several people from each village met to decide on conditions for a _____45_____ of peace to make sure that there would be no future wars between them.

B

People build homes out of whatever is around. In the United States, stone and wood are used a lot. Long ago, there used to be houses made of ice in the far north, and there still are houses made out of sun-baked mud in the hot and dry parts of the _____46_____ United States. Near the _____47_____, where the climate is warm and rainy, insects would damage wooden houses and stone is hard to find. In such _____48_____ areas, you may find instead houses that are built of plants. One fast growing family of plants that's often used is the _____49_____. These houses are a lot stronger than they look, being able to last through many, many storms. The one type of storm that can flatten them is a _____50_____, but then, wood and stone houses can be destroyed by such a fierce storm as well.

C

Once there was an old woman named Wendy who lived by herself in a little house near the edge of the great _____51_____. Since she had no one to keep her company, Wendy looked for a _____52_____ among the animals that lived nearby.

There was a large black cat who came to stay, and their _____53_____ made them both happy. And every so often a creature such as a bat, an owl, a toad, or an alligator came to visit as a _____54_____ and wound up moving in!

Soon the people in town began to say that Wendy could work magic spells. They were afraid, and one day they attacked her and tried to burn her house. In her _____55_____, Wendy changed them all into frogs and then flew off into the night on her broom.

D

Every so often, a _____56_____ is hurt or grows too old to hunt the other, swifter animals of the _____57_____. If human beings live nearby, it will learn to _____58_____ and kill the slow-moving humans instead.

These "man-eaters," as they are called, actually find it easier to attack a woman or a child in the field. But they also have been known to come right into a _____59_____ in the village and drag someone away. They kill men, too, of course. Even armed with a _____60_____, a man is an easy kill for this hunter.

—— **Check your answers with the key.** ——

beak (bēk), **1** bill of a bird. Eagles and hawks have strong, hooked beaks that are useful in striking or tearing. **2** anything shaped like a beak, such as the projecting prow of an ancient warship or the spout of a pitcher or jug. *noun.*

claw (klô), **1** a sharp, hooked nail on a bird's or animal's foot. **2** a foot with such sharp, hooked nails. **3** the pincers of a lobster or crab. **4** anything like a claw. The part of a hammer used for pulling nails is the claw. **5** scratch, tear, seize, or pull with claws or hands: *The kitten was clawing the screen door.* 1-4 *noun,* 5 *verb.*

dis turb (dis tėrb′), **1** destroy the peace, quiet, or rest of: *Heavy truck traffic disturbed the neighborhood.* **2** break in upon with noise; bother: *Please do not disturb her while she's studying.* **3** put out of order: *Someone has disturbed my books; I can't find the one I want.* **4** make uneasy; trouble: *He was disturbed to hear of his friend's illness.* *verb.*

flock (flok), **1** group of animals of one kind keeping, feeding, or herded together: *a flock of sheep, a flock of geese, a flock of birds.* **2** a large number; crowd: *Visitors came in flocks to the zoo to see the new gorilla.* **3** go in a flock; keep in groups: *Sheep usually flock together.* **4** people of the same church group. **5** come crowding; crowd: *The children flocked around the ice-cream stand.* 1,2,4 *noun,* 3,5 *verb.*

flut ter (flut′ər), **1** wave back and forth quickly and lightly: *The flag fluttered in the breeze.* **2** flap the wings; flap: *The chickens fluttered excitedly when they saw the dog.* **3** come or go with a trembling or wavy motion: *The falling leaves fluttered to the ground.* **4** move restlessly: *They fluttered about, making preparations for the party.* **5** beat a little faster than usual: *My heart fluttered when I rose to give my speech.* **6** fluttering: *the flutter of curtains in a breeze.* **7** excitement: *The appearance of the queen caused a great flutter in the crowd.* 1-5 *verb,* 6,7 *noun.*

geese (gēs), more than one goose. *noun plural.*

gig gle (gig′əl), **1** laugh in a silly or undignified way. **2** a silly or undignified laugh. 1 *verb,* **gig gled, gig gling;** 2 *noun.*

grum ble (grum′bəl), **1** complain in a rather sullen way; mutter in discontent; find fault: *The students are always grumbling about the cafeteria's food.* **2** mutter of discontent; bad-tempered complaint. **3** make a low, heavy sound like far-off thunder. 1,3 *verb,* **grum bled, grum bling;** 2 *noun.*

gull (gul), a graceful gray-and-white bird living on or near large bodies of water. A gull has long wings, webbed feet, and a thick, strong beak. *noun.*

mut ter (mut′ər), **1** speak or utter (words) low and indistinctly, with lips partly closed. **2** complain; grumble: *The shoppers muttered about the high price of meat.* **3** a low, indistinct sound: *We heard a mutter of discontent.* 1,2 *verb,* 3 *noun.*

par rot (par′ət), **1** bird with a stout, hooked bill and often with bright-colored feathers. Some parrots can imitate sounds and repeat words and sentences. **2** person who repeats words or acts without understanding them. *noun.*

pig eon (pij′ən), bird with a plump body and short legs; dove. *noun.*

rob in (rob′ən), **1** a large North American bird with a reddish breast. **2** a smaller European bird with an orange breast. *noun.*

squawk (skwôk), **1** make a loud, harsh sound: *Hens and ducks squawk when frightened.* **2** a loud, harsh sound. **3** complain loudly. **4** a loud complaint. 1,3 *verb,* 2,4 *noun.*

squeal (skwēl), **1** make a long, sharp, shrill cry: *A pig squeals when it is hurt.* **2** such a cry. **3** inform on another. 1,3 *verb,* 2 *noun.*

swan (swon), a large, graceful water bird with a long, slender, curving neck. The adult is usually pure white. *noun.*

swoop (swüp), **1** come down with a rush, as a hawk does; sweep rapidly down upon in a sudden attack: *Bats swooped down from the roof of the cave.* **2** a rapid downward sweep; sudden, swift descent or attack: *With one swoop the hawk seized the chicken and flew away.* **3** snatch: *The nurse swooped up the running child.* 1,3 *verb,* 2 *noun.*

trim (trim), **1** put in good order; make neat by cutting away parts: *The gardener trims the hedge. The barber trimmed my hair.* **2** neat; in good condition or order: *The entire family works together to keep a trim house.* **3** good condition or order: *Is our team in trim for the game?* **4** condition; order: *That ship is in poor trim for a voyage.* **5** decorate: *The children were trimming the Christmas tree.* **6** arrange (the sails) to fit wind and direction. **7** defeat; beat. 1,5-7 *verb,* **trimmed, trim ming;** 2 *adjective,* **trim mer, trim mest;** 3,4 *noun.*

un eas y (un ē′zē), **1** restless; disturbed; anxious. **2** not comfortable. **3** not easy in manner; awkward. *adjective,* **un eas i er, un eas i est.**

wood peck er (wùd′pek′ər), bird with a hard, pointed bill for pecking holes in trees to get insects. The flicker is one kind of woodpecker. *noun.*

Words in Sentences

Number from 1 to 20 on your answer sheet. Next to each numeral, write the word that belongs on that blank line in the sentence. Use the words at the left of each sentence. Use the Mini-Dictionary on the opposite page to find the meaning(s) of each word you don't know.

woodpecker _____
beak _____
mutter _____

When he heard the ____1____ loudly tapping its ____2____ against the tree, Bob began to ____3____ about getting out his gun.

grumble _____
parrot _____

Since it learned to talk, my ____4____ has done nothing but ____5____ about the food and say mean things about me.

claw _____
squeal _____
pigeon _____

The ____6____ gave a sharp ____7____ when the eagle's ____8____ dug into its back.

swoop _____
uneasy _____
robin _____

The little ____9____ in the tree seemed to be ____10____ until it saw another bird ____11____ down to the grass and begin hunting for worms.

trim _____
flutter _____
swan _____

The ____12____ bent its long neck and began to ____13____ its wings and pull at the loose feathers until each wing was neat and ____14____ again.

flock _____
squawk _____
geese _____

We heard one loud ____15____ from the gray goose and then a terrible cry as the whole ____16____ of ____17____ began to attack the dog.

giggle _____
disturb _____
gull _____

Some of the children began to laugh or ____18____ when the ____19____ flew down to join their picnic, but nothing seemed to ____20____ the hungry bird.

——— **Check your answers with the key.** ———

A

Number from 21 to 28 on your answer sheet. Next to each numeral, write the word from the box that has about the **same** meaning as the word(s) at the right.

beak	flock
grumble	trim
claw	giggle
uneasy	disturb

B

Number from 29 to 33 on your answer sheet. Next to each numeral, write the word from the box that completes the sentence.

swoop	squawk
mutter	flutter
squeal	

C

Number from 34 to 40 on your answer sheet. Next to each numeral, write the word from the box that completes the sentence.

woodpecker	swan
gull	robin
parrot	geese
pigeon	

A

21. nervous _____
22. a silly laugh _____
23. upset _____
24. cut short _____
25. find fault _____
26. crowd together _____
27. a bird's bill _____
28. dig with hands _____

—— **Check your answers with the key.** ——

B

29. horse : gallop : : butterfly : _____
30. take small bites : nibble : : tell on : _____
31. straw : hay : : complain : _____
32. hold back : control : : grab up : _____
33. sunshine : blizzard : : yell : _____

—— **Check your answers with the key.** ——

C

34. If it lives on the roofs of city buildings, it's probably a _____ .
35. If it lifts its long neck when it swims in the water, it's probably a _____ .
36. If it flies over the beach looking for food, it's probably a _____ .
37. If it can learn to talk, it's probably a _____ .
38. If it can bang a hole in a tree, it's probably a _____ .
39. If they get angry when you walk into the barnyard, they are probably _____ .
40. If its chest feathers are red and the rest is dull brown, it's probably a _____ .

—— **Check your answers with the key.** ——

84

Before you do the Words in Stories exercise, take the *Spelling Recognition Test* on page 146 and check your answers with the key at the back of the book.

 A

Number from 41 to 45 on your answer sheet. Next to each numeral, write the word from the box that completes the sentence.

beak	swan
flutter	woodpecker
robin	

B

Number from 46 to 50 on your answer sheet. Next to each numeral, write the word from the box that completes the sentence.

swoop	geese
pigeon	flock
disturb	

C

Number from 51 to 55 on your answer sheet. Next to each numeral, write the word from the box that completes the sentence.

parrot	squawk
claw	mutter
trim	

D

Number from 56 to 60 on your answer sheet. Next to each numeral, write the word from the box that completes the sentence.

grumble	giggle
squeal	gull
uneasy	

A

The zoo keepers at the Bird House are careful to give the wild birds the things they need. For the _____41_____ , there is a tree branch on which it can use its sharp _____42_____ to find insects. For the beautiful white _____43_____ , there is a pond in which it can swim and look for food. They also cut the bird's feathers every week so it can _____44_____ its great wings but cannot fly away.

On my last visit to the zoo I saw a little _____45_____ hopping along the grass looking for something to eat, but no one paid it any attention. For better or worse, it is free.

B

On a particular night you can see a certain _____46_____ of wild _____47_____ heading south for the winter. Every fall they _____48_____ down from the skies and come to rest on the quiet waters of the pond in our city park. Everyone is careful not to _____49_____ the proud, beautiful creatures. The only other bird the people will see outdoors before spring comes again will be the fat, noisy _____50_____ , looking for food.

C

Pete is a large, green and red _____51_____ who lives in a cage in Sylvia's room. Once a month she opens the door and tells Pete to step onto a stick she holds in her hand. Pete wraps his strong feet around the stick and Sylvia begins to _____52_____ each sharp, yellow _____53_____ while she talks to him.

Pete would never scratch her, but she doesn't understand that. She can't even speak clearly. She has to _____54_____ when she talks, which makes her hard to understand. She can't even make a short, sharp _____55_____ the way Pete can to get attention. But Pete is very patient with Sylvia. Little by little she is learning to speak like a regular bird!

D

The children run across the beach and bring pails of cold water back from the ocean. Some shout with laughter and others _____56_____ softly when the water is splashed on the sleeping grown-ups, who just _____57_____ and roll over again. Then the children dash off to the ocean and _____58_____ with excitement when the big waves knock them down.

All the while, the watchful _____59_____ moves a little closer to the beach blanket and the big picnic basket. The bird has learned the ways of these strange creatures by studying them. They are too slow to be dangerous, so there is no reason to feel _____60_____ . And inside that open basket is enough food to keep her alive for a week.

—— **Check your answers with the key.** ——

bur ro (bėr′ō), a small donkey used to carry loads or packs in the southwestern United States. *noun, plural* **bur ros.**

can yon (kan′yən), a narrow valley with high, steep sides, usually with a stream at the bottom. *noun.*

car pen ter (kär′pən tər), person whose work is building and repairing the wooden parts of houses, barns, and ships. *noun.*

coy o te (kī ō′tē *or* kī′ōt), a small wolflike animal living on the prairies of western North America. *noun, plural* **coy o tes** *or* **coy o te.**

firm[1] (fėrm), **1** not yielding when pressed: *firm flesh, firm ground.* **2** solid; fixed in place; not easily shaken or moved: *a tree firm in the earth.* **3** not easily changed; determined; positive: *a firm voice, a firm character, a firm belief. adjective.*

firm[2] (fėrm), company of two or more persons in business together. *noun.*

fron tier (frun tir′), **1** the last edge of settled country, where the wilds begin. **2** part of one country that touches the edge of another; boundary line between two countries. **3** an uncertain or undeveloped region: *explore the frontiers of science. noun.*

howl (houl), **1** give a long, loud, mournful cry: *Our dog often howls at night. The winter winds howled around our cabin.* **2** a long, loud, mournful cry: *the howl of a wolf.* **3** give a long, loud cry of pain or rage. **4** a loud cry of pain or rage. **5** a yell or shout: *We heard howls of laughter.* **6** yell or shout: *It was so funny that we howled with laughter.* **7** force or drive by howling: *The angry mob howled the speaker off the platform.* 1,3,6,7 *verb,* 2,4,5 *noun.*

lone some (lōn′səm), **1** feeling lonely: *I was lonesome while you were away.* **2** making one feel lonely: *a lonesome journey. adjective,* **lone som er, lone som est.**

me sa (mā′sə), a high, steep hill that has a flat top and stands alone. A mesa is usually larger and steeper than a butte. *noun.* [*Mesa* comes from a Latin word meaning "table."]

mes sen ger (mes′n jər), person who carries a message or goes on an errand. *noun.*

part ner (pärt′nər), **1** one who shares: *My sister was the partner of my walks.* **2** member of a company or firm who shares the risks and profits of the business. **3** wife or husband. **4** companion in a dance. **5** player on the same team or side in a game. *noun.*

pi o neer (pī′ə nir′), **1** person who settles in a part of a country, preparing it for others. **2** person who goes first, or does something first, and so prepares a way for others: *a pioneer in medical science.* **3** prepare or open up for others; take the lead: *Astronauts are pioneering in exploring outer space.* 1,2 *noun,* 3 *verb.*

prair ie (prer′ē), a large area of level or rolling land with grass but few or no trees. *noun.*

roam (rōm), go about with no special plan or aim; wander: *roam through the fields. verb.*

rude (rüd), **1** impolite; not courteous: *It is rude to stare at people or to point.* **2** rough; coarse; roughly made or done: *Prehistoric people made rude tools from stone.* **3** very forceful; violent; rough in manner or behavior: *Rude hands seized the barking dog.* **4** not having learned much; primitive: *Rude tribes lived in the jungle surrounding the river. adjective,* **rud er, rud est.**

ru in (rü′ən), **1** building or wall that has fallen to pieces: *That ruin was once a famous castle.* **2** very great damage; destruction; overthrow: *The ruin of property caused by the earthquake was enormous. His enemies planned the duke's ruin.* **3** a fallen or decayed condition: *The house had gone to ruin from neglect.* **4** cause of destruction, decay, or downfall: *Reckless spending will be your ruin.* **5** destroy; spoil: *The rain ruined our picnic.* 1-4 *noun,* 5 *verb.*

rus tle (rus′əl), **1** a light, soft sound of things gently rubbing together. **2** make or cause to make this sound: *Leaves rustled in the breeze. The wind rustled the papers.* **3** steal (cattle or horses). 1 *noun,* 2,3 *verb,* **rus tled, rus tling.**

sav age (sav′ij), **1** member of a primitive, uncivilized people. **2** not civilized: *savage customs.* **3** fierce; cruel; ready to fight: *a savage dog.* **4** a fierce, brutal, or cruel person. **5** wild or rugged: *savage mountain scenery.* 1,4 *noun,* 2,3,5 *adjective.*

set tler (set′lər), **1** person who settles. **2** person who settles in a new country. *noun.*

sher iff (sher′if), the most important law-enforcing officer of a county. A sheriff appoints deputies who help to keep order. *noun.*

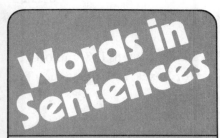

A

Number from 1 to 20 on your answer sheet. Next to each numeral, write the word that belongs on that blank line in the sentence. Use the words at the left of each sentence. Use the Mini-Dictionary on the opposite page to find the meaning(s) of each word you don't know.

burro

pioneer

canyon

Riding the little ___1___ across the floor of the ___2___ made Susan feel like the ___3___ who had first traveled through these lands.

howl

coyote

mesa

On the flat top of the ___4___ , you could see the shape of a ___5___ lifting its nose to ___6___ at the moon.

prairie

ruin

lonesome

When I see the ___7___ of an old farmhouse out on the empty ___8___ , I get a ___9___ feeling.

sheriff

frontier

rustle

On the western ___10___ , a man who tried to ___11___ another man's cattle might be hanged, even before the ___12___ could arrest him.

roam

messenger

firm

The ___13___ who works for our banking ___14___ is bright and quick, but she likes to ___15___ around the city each time she carries a message.

savage

partner

rude

Mike is a gentle man with fine manners, but his ___16___ , Wild Bill, is ___17___ to people and becomes a ___18___ fighter when he gets angry.

settler

carpenter

Each new ___19___ in the valley was expected to build his own cabin and learn to become a ___20___ as well as a farmer.

—— **Check your answers with the key.** ——

Word Play

A

Number from 21 to 25 on your answer sheet. Next to each numeral, write the word from the box that completes the sentence.

partner	**mesa**
carpenter	**sheriff**
settler	

B

Number from 26 to 34 on your answer sheet. Next to each numeral, write the word from the box that means about the **same** as the word(s) at the right.

rustle	**canyon**
rude	**pioneer**
savage	**roam**
ruin	**lonesome**
howl	

C

Number from 35 to 40 on your answer sheet. Next to each numeral, write the word from the box that completes the group.

firm	**frontier**
messenger	**coyote**
prairie	**burro**

A

21. In the west, it's the _____ who keeps law and order.
22. A _____ builds houses or boxes, as long as they are made of wood.
23. A _____ is a companion during a dance.
24. A _____ is tall and stands alone.
25. A _____ goes to live in a new country.

—— **Check your answers with the key.** ——

B

26. lead the way
27. long, loud cry
28. light, soft sound
29. great damage
30. wander
31. lonely
32. fierce
33. not polite
34. narrow valley

—— **Check your answers with the key.** ——

C

35. huge : enormous : : plain : _____
36. tiger : cat : : donkey : _____
37. tame : dog : : wild : _____
38. guest : visitor : : company : _____
39. center : middle : : edge : _____
40. cargo : ship : : message : _____

—— **Check your answers with the key.** ——

Before you do the Words in Stories exercise, take the *Spelling Recognition Test* on page 147 and check your answers with the key at the back of the book.

Number from 41 to 45 on your answer sheet. Next to each numeral, write the word from the box that completes the sentence.

messenger	frontier
firm	sheriff
savage	

B

Number from 46 to 50 on your answer sheet. Next to each numeral, write the word from the box that completes the sentence.

rude	settler
carpenter	prairie
lonesome	

C

Number from 51 to 55 on your answer sheet. Next to each numeral, write the word from the box that completes the sentence.

mesa	howl
ruin	rustle
coyote	

D

Number from 56 to 60 on your answer sheet. Next to each numeral, write the word from the box that completes the sentence.

roam	partner
canyon	pioneer
burro	

A

The streets of the wild ____41____ town were empty. There was a showdown coming and no one wanted to be outside.

Suddenly a ____42____ dashed across the street and slipped inside the office of the town ____43____ . The man carried a warning note. Big Bertha had just stepped off the train!

It was time. The man who stood for law and order put on his guns and pinned his star to his chest. He tried to keep his step ____44____ and his hands from shaking. Bertha was the fastest and most ____45____ fighter he had ever met. He had been married to her for twenty years and he hadn't won a showdown yet!

B

The new man who has begun to build a house on that land is no ____46____ . He can hardly use a saw to cut the wood. But he has managed to put in a floor and raise the walls of a ____47____ log cabin. When it is time to add the roof, each ____48____ for miles around will come to help. One more family, coming to live on the huge, empty ____49____ , would make it a little less ____50____ for the others.

C

Bob had been in charge of a children's TV show where everyone talked and acted like animals. But now he was out of work. The fact that people didn't watch "talking animals" on TV anymore had been Bob's ____51____ .

Bob lived by himself on a ranch. It was so quiet there, you could hear the wind ____52____ the leaves in the trees.

One night when the moon was full, Bob packed a bag and drove out to the base of the big red ____53____ . He climbed to the top and took an old ____54____ skin out of the bag and threw it over his shoulders. Bob thought again of how rich and famous he had once been. He lifted his face to the sky and let out a long, sad ____55____ .

D

Pat had been Nancy's ____56____ ever since they'd found their "secret" place. On their first trip into the mountains, they'd found a hidden ____57____ where Nancy was sure they would find gold. So each spring they loaded up a ____58____ and set out on their search.

Pat was pretty sure they'd never strike it rich, but she enjoyed escaping from her everyday life once a year to ____59____ the wild hills and valleys. Pat and Nancy wanted to live in the rough and rocky hill country. Each woman had the spark of a true ____60____ .

—— **Check your answers with the key.** ——

Review Lesson

Choose the word from each pair that best completes the sentence.

A

1. sheriff	2. companion
3. royal	4. aye
5. league	6. frontier
7. canyon	8. pirate
9. woodpecker	10. coyote
11. prairie	12. pioneer
13. mutter	14. howl
15. giggle	16. awkward
17. settler	18. anger
19. treaty	20. dignity
21. claw	22. savage
23. roam	24. rustle
25. Eskimo	26. Eastern
27. partner	28. warrior
29. battle	30. disturb
31. firm	32. spear
33. blubber	34. guest

B

35. zone	36. neighborhood
37. reindeer	38. geese
39. burro	40. swan
41. stalk	42. paddle
43. lonesome	44. stern
45. oar	46. pigeon
47. walrus	48. robin
49. beak	50. mesa
51. furnace	52. refrigerator
53. grumble	54. trim
55. landlord	56. messenger
57. bare	58. rude
59. flock	60. temperature
61. gradually	62. icy
63. cargo	64. suitcase
65. hunger	66. friendship

A

Clive Henry was an Englishman who had come to visit the Wild West during the 1870s. Since Clive was a close ____ 1 or 2 ____ of the King of England, and since he planned to marry into the ____ 3 or 4 ____ family, he was very correct in his speech and his dress. But Clive loved the life on the ____ 5 or 6 ____ . He said he had never seen anything as beautiful as the colored rocks on the sides of a western ____ 7 or 8 ____ . He even loved to hear the sound of a lonely ____ 9 or 10 ____ at night.

However, Clive didn't meet a single ____ 11 or 12 ____ who was pleased to see him. "He's no real man," they would ____ 13 or 14 ____ to themselves. "He doesn't even laugh like a man. His laugh sounds more like a ____ 15 or 16 ____ . He never gets angry like a man. There's no ____ 17 or 18 ____ in him. He's just a stuffed shirt with too much ____ 19 or 20 ____ ."

Finally, Clive ran up against a cold-eyed man who was known as one of the most ____ 21 or 22 ____ gunfighters around. "I'm the meanest so-and-so in these parts!" the man shouted. "Every morning before breakfast I ____ 23 or 24 ____ a few head of cattle just to start the day right. And one thing I can't stand is a fancy-pants ____ 25 or 26 ____ type like you. Reach for your gun!"

From the corner of his eye, Clive saw the man's ____ 27 or 28 ____ moving around behind him. The Englishman saw that he'd have to do ____ 29 or 30 ____ immediately. Clive swiftly drew his guns and shot the guns out of both men's hands. "Every morning the King and I shoot a dozen fat, silly birds before breakfast just to start the day right," Clive said in his ____ 31 or 32 ____ , pleasant voice. "If I were you, I would be more polite when meeting a man who is a ____ 33 or 34 ____ in your country."

B

The kids in the ____ 35 or 36 ____ called Laura the "Bird Lady." Each day Laura spent hours watching the ____ 37 or 38 ____ in the little pond in our city park. And she loved to watch the white ____ 39 or 40 ____ . It would ____ 41 or 42 ____ toward her when she threw food on the water.

When some of her feathered friends flew south for the winter, Laura wasn't too ____ 43 or 44 ____ . She'd give pieces of bread to each ____ 45 or 46 ____ that stayed in the city. And each spring a ____ 47 or 48 ____ would return in search of the food she left for it. She loved to watch it carefully pick up each piece of bread in its ____ 49 or 50 ____ .

Lately though, the winters were getting harder for Laura. The ____ 51 or 52 ____ kept breaking down and it was just too cold to get out of bed in the morning. Laura would ____ 53 or 54 ____ regularly, but it took the ____ 55 or 56 ____ a very long time to fix anything, and he was always very unfriendly and ____ 57 or 58 ____ . Meanwhile, the ____ 59 or 60 ____ inside the apartment was ____ 61 or 62 ____ cold. There was only one thing to do, Laura decided. She packed a ____ 63 or 64 ____ and flew south for the winter. She was looking for the same thing her bird friends were looking for—a little ____ 65 or 66 ____ and a warm place in the sun!

Review Lesson

C

67. voyage	68. equator
69. blizzard	70. hurricane
71. northern	72. southern
73. surround	74. swoop
75. ruin	76. squeal
77. tropical	78. polar
79. gull	80. kayak
81. mast	82. crew
83. carpenter	84. anchor
85. deal	86. glow
87. wharf	88. hut
89. tiger	90. tide
91. swamp	92. seaport
93. uneasy	94. shallow
95. bamboo	96. parrot
97. squawk	98. flutter
99. navy	100. jungle

C

For two days and nights the little island below the _____67 or 68_____ had been sent _____69 or 70_____ warnings. In those _____71 or 72_____ seas, a storm can take days to build up before it begins to move. Then it can change direction suddenly and _____73 or 74_____ down to _____75 or 76_____ everything in its path.

On the island, the hot air was heavy and still along the _____77 or 78_____ beach. There wasn't a single _____79 or 80_____ or other creature to be seen. To get ready for the storm, the _____81 or 82_____ of the large ship pulled up the _____83 or 84_____ and took the ship further out to sea. Now it would be safe from the pounding waves near shore.

Soon the sky turned a dull gray, and the sun seemed to _____85 or 86_____ with an angry red color. The angry-looking waves began breaking over the top of the long _____87 or 88_____ , even though it should have been low _____89 or 90_____ . Everywhere in the small _____91 or 92_____ the people waited in _____93 or 94_____ silence. Suddenly, the wind shifted. A _____95 or 96_____ gave one shrill _____97 or 98_____ somewhere deep in the _____99 or 100_____ , and then all life on the island was at the mercy of the fierce winds.

—— **Check your answers with the key.** ——

Why is good spelling important? If you are a student, good spelling is important in all of the writing you do. Outside of school, good spelling will help you in getting and keeping a job, placing orders, filling out applications, and in many more ways.

In any kind of writing, poor spelling causes misunderstanding. No matter what you write, you are trying to tell someone something that you feel is important. If you spell correctly, your message has a better chance of being understood.

People often judge you by how well you can spell. Whether you are working or going to school, good spelling can make quite a difference. People feel that a good speller has "more on the ball" than someone who won't take the trouble to spell well.

There is no such thing as a perfect speller. That is because the English language has many ways of spelling the same sound. Even good spellers have to check their spelling of some words.

Whether you are a good, average, or poor speller, you can become better.

Nine Ways to Be a Better Speller

1. You have to want to be a good speller. You have to make up your mind that your are going to try hard. There is no way for lazy people to learn to spell well.
2. You have to be able to pronounce words. This means that you need to know the difference between vowels and consonants. You must also know the different ways that vowels and consonants are used together to make different sounds. For help in sounding out words, read "Help in Sounding Out Words" beginning on this page.
3. You have to be able to break words into syllables. A syllable is a part of a word that has one vowel sound. For example, the word "example" has three syllables: ex-am-ple. For help in breaking words into syllables, turn to page 94.
4. Pay special attention to words that have endings that change. Help in changing word endings can be found on pages 94-95.
5. Two letters that cause many spelling problems are **i** and **e** when found together.
   A rule that helps with that problem is found in this rhyme:

   i before **e**
   Except after **c**,
   Or when sounded as **ay**
   (As in **neighbor** or **weigh**).

Notice how this rule works with words like *believe* and *receive*. However, no rule works all the time. Here are some words with which this rule does *not* work:

leisure	seize
neither	weird

6. Watch out for homonyms. These are pairs of words that sound the same but have different spellings and meanings. *Maid* and *made* are examples of homonyms. In the word list that starts on page 97, you'll find the most common homonyms and their meanings.
7. You have to develop a good "visual memory." This means you have a picture in your mind of the correct spelling of many words. Training with the Tach-X and Flash-X will help you improve your visual memory.
8. Never guess at words. Good spellers always look up words they are not sure they know. If you use the wrong spelling for a word, it may become a habit. If you are not sure of a word's spelling, look it up in a dictionary or in one of the two word lists in this book. One list gives the 400 words in this program in alphabetical order. The second list, also alphabetical, contains hard words that most people have trouble spelling.
9. Whenever you write, use good spelling. Some people feel that good spelling is just getting 100 on a spelling test. Good spelling is more than this. Really good spellers are careful whenever they write something that another person is going to read. When you have finished writing something, read through it carefully, watching for spelling mistakes (and other errors, too). This is called "proofreading."

Help in Sounding Out Words

Consonants

Consonants can appear at the beginning, middle, and end of words.

b	bus	robin	tub
c	cash	because	
c	cent	decide	lace
d	day	ladder	sad
f	for	offer	if
g	go	begin	hug
g	gentle	huge	
h	help	behold	

j	job	just	
k	keep	back	
l	let	allow	ill
m	men	hammer	swim
n	no	banana	can
p	pay	slipper	drip
q	quiet	quick	
r	ride	arrow	far
s	see	trees	
t	talk	letter	cat
v	very	over	love
w	women	away	
y	yes	beyond	
z	zoo	amaze	

Consonant Blends

Consonants can be put together to make consonant blends. In a consonant blend, you hear the sounds of two or more consonants. Some of the most common consonant blends are shown in these words:

black, brave

class, crack

drip

flat, fresh

glad, great

plan, pride

sleep, small, snow, spot, spray, stop, street

tree

Consonant blends also come at the ends of words, like this:

tent, ask, help

Consonant Digraphs

Consonant digraphs are different from consonant blends. In a consonant digraph, the letter h is placed after c, s, t, or w to produce a new sound, as in:

chair, shop, that, why

Consonant digraphs also appear at the ends of words, such as:

each, dish, with

Unusual Consonant Sounds

English is a funny language. Sometimes two consonants make a sound that is completely different from the sounds of the individual letters. Here are some of these different sounds:

ph sounds like f in graph

gh sounds like f in rough

ch sounds like k in ache

Short Vowel Sounds		Long Vowel, Silent Final e	
a	at	a	came
e	bed	e	scene
i	it	i	ride
o	on	o	home
u	us	u	June

Long Vowel, Two Vowels Together		Exceptions	
a	rain	bread, head	
e	heat	great, steak	
i	tie		
o	coat		
u	true		

Other Long Vowel Sounds

y with long i sound: by, my, why

y with long e sound: very, city, puppy

ay with long a sound: may, say, tray

ew with long u sound: few, chew

ow with long o sound: blow, snow

R-Controlled Sounds

ar: far

or: for

er: her

ir: girl } Notice that er, ir, and

ur: burn } ur have the same sound.

Vowel Digraphs

Vowel digraphs are combinations of letters in which you can hear two vowel sounds.

ow: how, cow, now } Notice that ow and ou

ou: about, found } have the same sound.

oi: point, voice } Notice that oi and oy

oy: boy, enjoy } have the same sound.

Three Sounds of oo

school, roof, goose

book, look, good

blood, flood

One Sound for au, aw

draw, saw, jaw, pause, cause

How to Break Words into Syllables

One Vowel Sound to Each Syllable

The most important thing to know about breaking words into syllables is that each syllable has one vowel sound.

Hop has one syllable.
Pen/cil has two syllables.
Ra/di/o and el/e/phant have three syllables.
Au/to/mo/bile and un/der/stand/ing have four syllables.

Patterns for Breaking Words into Syllables

Most two-syllable words fall into three major patterns.

1. Break between two consonants
   rab/bit   pic/nic
   This also applies to blends and digraphs.
   com/plain   birth/day
2. Break after a long-vowel syllable
   to/day be/fore re/turn
3. Break after consonant when first syllable has a short vowel sound
   cab/in   riv/er

Breaking Longer Words into Syllables

With longer words, listen for the vowel sounds. Make sure you have a vowel sound in each syllable.

au/to/mo/bile   un/der/stand/ing

How to Change Word Endings

When you write something, there will be times when you know a word, but you want to use it in a different way. You may know the word "library," but you want to write about more than one library. You may know how to say "I dance," but you don't know how to say it when it happened yesterday. Here are some ways to change words to make them say different things.

Adding s and es to Nouns

1. When there is more than one, and you want to write the plural of a noun, you add **s** to some words.

   | one ladder | two ladders |
   | one grape | two grapes |

2. With some words, you add **es** to make the plurals.

   | stitch | stitches |
   | ax | axes |

3. When the word ends with **y**, you change **y** to **i** and add **es** to form a plural.

   | one hobby | two hobbies |
   | one army | two armies |

Adding s, es, and ies to Verbs

You do the same thing with verbs (words that tell what people do).

When I, we, you, or they do something:	When he, she, or it does something:
I run	it runs
we run	she runs
you watch	he watches
they watch	she watches
I study	he studies
we study	she studies

Adding ing to Verbs

1. For many words, you add **ing** without making a change.

   | chew | chewing |
   | worry | worrying |

2. When a word ends in a consonant with one vowel before it, you double the consonant.

   | split | splitting |
   | begin | beginning |

3. When a word ends in **e**, you drop the **e** before adding **ing**.

breathe	breathing
serve	serving
blame	blaming

Adding d, ed to Verbs

1. When a word ends in **e**, we just add **d** to show that something has happened.

   | admire | admired |
   | care | cared |

2. For many words, we add **ed** without making a change.

   | scream | screamed |
   | report | reported |

3. When a word ends in **y**, we change **y** to **i** and add **ed**.

   | satisfy | satisfied |
   | marry | married |

4. When a word ends in a consonant with one vowel before it, we double the consonant and add **ed**.

stop   stopped
plan   planned

How This Program Will Help

The spelling part of the Language Clues Program will help you become a better speller in these ways:

1. At the end of every Language Clues lesson, you will find out which words you have trouble spelling. You will put these words on a special spelling list.
2. You will study your hard words. Two ways to study words are given in the next section.
3. After five Language Clues lessons, you will be tested on all of the words in those five lessons. You'll make another list of hard words.
4. Your teacher will help you decide what kind of spelling help you need:

   - Help in hearing the sounds in words
   - Help in remembering spelling patterns
   - Help in remembering how words look

How to Study Your Hard Words

After each Language Clues lesson, your own hard words will show up on your spelling paper. This paper will give the correct spelling of each of your hard words.

Here are two ways to study your hard words.

With Paper and Pencil

Take a fresh piece of lined paper and make a list of your hard words. Number each word and be sure to spell it correctly. Write neatly so that each letter is clear.

You will also need:

- A card for covering words
- A pencil
- Another piece of paper

You will use the card as a shutter to uncover and cover each word.

1. Place the card so that its top covers the first word on your list. If you are right-handed, hold the card in your left hand. If you are left-handed, hold the card in your right hand.
2. Uncover the first word quickly. Look at all the letters. Then cover it up again.
3. Say the word. Hear every syllable.
4. Write the word. Say it as you write it.
5. Check the word by uncovering it with the card. If you made any mistakes, circle the parts that were wrong. Then write the word again, correctly.
6. Looking away from the word, say it to yourself. Try to see a picture of the word in your mind's eye.
7. Then write the word again and check it.

Practice with your hard words until you are sure of their spelling. Then ask your teacher to check you on these words.

With Another Student

You will need:

- A pencil
- A piece of paper

Ask the other student to dictate your hard words to you. Check the spelling of each word right after you write it. If you get a word wrong, that word should be repeated until you get it right.

Take turns. Dictate the other student's hard words to her or him.

accident
accuse
ache
acre
acrobat
action
actor
actually
admire
admit
afford
agree
alligator
amount
ancestor
anchor
ancient
anger
appearance
area
argue
arrangement
arrest
artist
astronaut
attention
August
avenue
avoid
awkward
Aye
bamboo
bare
battery
battle
beak
beef
blizzard
blubber
brass
breathe
buck
buckle
bullet
burro
burst
bushel
business
canyon
capture
cargo
carpenter
cast
celebrate
champion
character
cheerful
chore
claw
collect
collection
colonel
command
committee
companion
condition
control
convenient
corral

cot
cotton
court
coyote
creature
crew
crocodile
crop
cub
cure
curiosity
customer
damage
dangerous
death
December
declare
defend
delivery
demand
department
detective
develop
difficult
dignity
discovery
disease
disgrace
distance
disturb
doubt
dozen
dreadful
dull
earthquake
eastern
eighteen
eighth
enemy
engineer
enormous
envelope
equal
equator
Eskimo
examination
examine
expensive
experiment
expert
explanation
explode
eyebrow
eyelash
eyelid
fact
familiar
figure
final
firm
fist
flare
flavor
flicker
flight
flock
flood
flute
flutter

fort
fortunate
freedom
friendship
frontier
frozen
furnace
future
gallop
geese
general
ghost
giggle
gloomy
glow
government
grade
gradually
groan
grumble
guest
guitar
gull
habit
harvest
health
heap
hesitate
hitch
hobby
honest
horrify
hotel
howl
human
hunger
hurricane
hut
icy
imitate
immediately
impatient
improve
improvement
information
insist
instant
instrument
interrupt
invent
invention
jail
January
jeep
jungle
kayak
landlord
league
leather
length
level
lip
lonesome
magazine
magician
mare
married
mast
material

measure
medal
medicine
mesa
messenger
midnight
million
modern
motion
movies
music
musician
mustache
mutter
mysterious
mystery
national
natural
nature
navy
necessary
neighborhood
nephew
nervous
news
newspaper
nineteen
ninth
noon
northern
nurse
oar
obey
October
officer
opposite
orbit
orchard
ordinary
paddle
pain
pants
paragraph
parrot
particular
partner
patient
pause
peace
peaceful
pear
perfect
perform
person
pigeon
pioneer
pirate
planet
platform
poison
polar
popular
position
possession
possibly
prairie
praise
preparation
prison

prisoner
private
professor
program
protect
protection
punish
pupil
purpose
quarrel
quart
quarter
rare
realize
refrigerator
regular
reindeer
remind
report
responsible
rifle
rise
roam
robin
rocket
rodeo
rough
royal
rude
ruin
rustle
saddle
salute
savage
scientist
score
screech
scythe
seal
seaport
September
settler
seventeen
seventh
shallow
shark
shelter
shepherd
sheriff
shift
shiver
shoulder
shove
silence
siren
sixth
sleeve
slender
soar
soldier
sour
southern
spear
squawk
squeal
stable
stalk
stallion
steady

stern
stolen
stomach
strength
succeed
suggest
suitcase
supplies
support
surface
surrender
surround
suspect
swamp
swan
swoop
tame
telescope
temperature
terror
thankful
threaten
thrifty
tide
tiger
treaty
trim
tropical
trumpet
Tuesday
twelfth
uneasy
uniform
upset
vanish
victory
volcano
voyage
waist
walrus
warrior
weary
Wednesday
weed
western
wharf
wheelbarrow
wigwam
woodpecker
wound
wrist
yell
yesterday
zero
zone

A accept
  Accept a gift.
ache
advice
  Take my advice.
advise
  I advise you.
affect
  It will affect me.
again
air
  fresh air
aisle
  down the aisle
alley
  in the alley
all right
ally
  an ally in war
aloud
  Read aloud.
altar
  at the altar
alter
  Alter my plans.
always
am
among
an
and
angel
  Be an angel.
angle
  a sharp angle
animals
another
answer
ant
  a crawling ant
any
are
  We are here.
around
asked
ate
  He ate supper.
aunt
  My aunt is sick.
aye
  The sailor said "aye."

B babies

bail
  Bail the boat.
bale
  bale of cotton

bare
  The trees are bare.
base
  first base
bass
  Sing bass. Catch a bass.
be
  Be good.
bear
  black bear
beat
  Beat the rug.
beau
  He is my beau.
beautiful
because
bee
  bee sting
been
  He has been here.
beets
  Pass the beets.
before
beginning
believe
berry
  a red berry
berth
  a lower berth
bin
  a bin of flour
birth
  the baby's birth
birthday
blew
  The wind blew.
blue
  the blue sky
board
  Cut the board.
boarder
  a boarder at our house
border
  across the border
bore
  It will bore you.
born
  born long ago
borne
  He has borne it well.
bough
  bough of a tree
bought
bow
  a polite bow; a ribbon bow
brake
  Brake the car.

bread
  loaf of bread
break
  Break a dish.
bred
  well bred
brew
  Brew some tea.
bridle
  the horse's bridle
brow
  a heavy brow
browse
  Browse in the store.
bruise
  a bad bruise
built
bury
  Bury the body.
business
busy
but
  all but me
butt
  Butt with the head.
buy
  Buy a gift.
by
  by the sea

C cache
  a secret cache
came
can't
capital
  capital letter
capitol
  capitol building
cash
  Pay cash.
caught
cell
  prison cell
cent
  one-cent stamp
cereal
  Eat your cereal.
children
choose
  Choose me.
chord
  musical chord
chose
  Last week I chose him.
Christmas
chute
  laundry chute

clause
clause in a sentence

claw
the cat's claw

cloth
Sew the cloth.

clothes
Put on clothes.

coarse
coarse thread

colonel
colonel in the army

color

coming

cord
Tie the cord.

core
an apple core

corps
the marine corps

corpse
Bury the corpse.

corral
animal corral

cough

could

council
The council will decide.

counsel
I need your counsel.

country

county

course
Of course I will.

cousin

criticize

cruise
cruise ship

D **daze**
in a daze

dear
a dear child

decent
a decent mark

decided

deer
The deer ran.

descent
The descent was steep.

desert
lost in the desert

dessert
apple pie for dessert

dew
dew on the grass

didn't

die
die of old age

different

do
I can do it.

doctor

does

doesn't

done

don't

dose
dose of medicine

down

doze
nod and doze

dropped

dual
dual purpose

due
He is due soon.

duel
Duel with swords.

dye
Dye it red.

E **early**

earn
Earn money.

easy

eight
eight o'clock

enough

every

except
all except one

eye
He hurt his eye.

F **fair**
Go to the fair.

fairy
fairy princess

fare
The fare is 5¢.

feat
a great feat

February

feet
His feet are wet.

ferry
ferry boat

finally

fine

fir
fir tree

first

flea
flea on the dog

flee
Flee quickly!

flew
The birds flew.

flour
baking flour

flower
the pretty flower

flue
chimney flue

for
Sing for me.

fore
to the fore

forth
back and forth

forty

foul
foul ball

four
four o'clock

fourth
in fourth place

fowl
Hens are fowl.

friend

frightened

from

fur
fur coat

G **gait**
the horse's gait

gale
gale winds

gate
garden gate

getting

gilt
a gilt edge

goes

going

good-by

grammar

grate
a grate in the fireplace

great
a great big elephant

groan
a loud groan

grown
a grown man

guessed
He guessed right.

guest
He is our guest.
guilt
guilt of the criminal

H **hail**
rain and hail
hair
Her hair is red.
half
Halloween
hangar
airplane hangar
hanger
coat hanger
happened
hare
A hare is like a rabbit.
have
haven't
having
he
hear
I hear you.
heard
I heard you.
heel
heel of a shoe
heir
heir to the throne
herd
herd of cows
here
Here we are.
higher
to jump higher
him
I see him.
hire
boat for hire
hoard
Hoard the money.
hoarse
hoarse voice
hole
hole in his shoe
holy
a holy place
horde
a horde of insects
horse
Ride a horse.
hour
The hour is late.
how
hymn
Sing a hymn.

I **I**
I am here.
idle
idle hours
idol
idol of his family
I'll
I'm
immediately
in
in the way
inn
Stay at the inn.
instead
isle
isle in the ocean
it
its
in its place
it's
It's two o'clock.

J **jumped**
just

K **kernel**
kernel of corn
knead
Knead the dough.
knew
He knew it.
knight
the gallant knight
knot
knot in the string
know
I know it.

L **laid**
He laid the book down.
lair
wolf's lair
lane
country lane
layer
layer of rocks
lead
lead pencil; I will lead.
led
He was led out.
lessen
Lessen the blow.
lesson
school lesson
let's
let us
letter

levee
a river levee
levy
to levy taxes
library
lie
to lie down
like
little
loan
loan of money
lone
lone wolf
looked
loose
The rope is loose.
lose
Don't lose it.
lye
Soap contains lye.

M **made**
I made a cake.
maid
The maid served lunch.
mail
Mail the letters.
main
the main street
making
male
The cat is a male.
mane
horse's mane
manner
a polite manner
manor
the lord of the manor
mantel
a mantel above the fireplace
mantle
wearing a mantle
many
march
March in line.
March
month of March
mare
"old gray mare"
may
You may go.
May
month of May
mayor
mayor of the town
me
meant

meat
Beef is meat.
medal
He won a medal.
meddle
Don't meddle.
meet
Meet me there.
miner
coal miner
minor
minor problem
minute
miss
Miss the train.
Miss
Miss Jones
mist
a wet mist
money
moral
a moral issue
morale
the soldier's morale
morning
early in the morning
mother
mourn
to mourn in grief
move
Mrs.
much
my

N **name**
named
necessary
need
I need help.
new
new shoes
no
He said, "No."
none
None was left.
nose
a large nose
not
I will not go.
now

O **oar**
rowboat oar
occurred
o'clock
of
one of them

off
off and on
often
oh
Oh, no!
omit
on
once
one
one o'clock
or
one or the other
ore
iron ore
our
our book
owe
I owe you.

P **pail**
pail and shovel
pain
ache and pain
pair
pair of socks
pale
pale color
pane
window pane
parallel
pare
pare the apple
past
past and present
pause
a short pause
peace
peace and quiet
peak
mountain peak
peal
The bells peal.
pear
a ripe pear
pedal
foot pedal
peddle
to peddle wares
peek
Peek in the window.
peel
Peel the apple.
peer
Peer at the girl.
people
perhaps
piece
piece of pie

pier
ship at the pier
plain
plain water
plane
plane in the sky
play
pleasant
pole
telephone pole
poll
to take a poll
pore
pore in the skin
pour
to pour water
praise
He should get praise.
precede
I will precede you in line.
presence
Her presence is known.
presents
birthday presents
pretty
prey
the lion's prey
principal
principal of the school
principle
A principle is a rule.
proceed
Proceed with the lesson.
prove

Q **quiet**
a quiet room
quite
quite new

R **rain**
rain and snow
raise
read
Read a book today.
We read yesterday.
ready
real
the real thing
realize
really
receive
red
The color is red.
reed
a reed by the lake
reel
fishing reel

reign
The king will reign.
reins
reins on a horse
right
right and left
road
the open road
rode
He rode away.
role
a leading role
roll
Roll down the hill.
root
root of the plant
route
route for the trip
running

S **said**
sail
Sail a boat.
sale
for sale
Saturday
says
scene
a pretty scene
scent
scent of perfume
school
sea
Sail on the sea.
seam
seam of a dress
see
I see you.
seem
They seem small.
seems
seen
I have seen him.
seize
Seize the ship!
sell
Sell the car.
sense
common sense
sent
He sent a note.
separate
serial
story in serial form
sew
Sew the button.
shear
Shear the sheep.

sheer
sheer stockings
shoes
sight
a beautiful sight
similar
since
site
building site
slay
Slay the dragon.
sleigh
sleigh ride
so
He is so big.
soar
See the plane soar.
sole
the sole guest
some
Have some candy.
something
sometimes
son
son and daughter
sore
a sore throat
soul
heart and soul
sow
Sow seeds.
stairs
up the stairs
stake
a wooden stake
stare
Stare at the picture.
started
stationary
stationary furniture
stationery
Write on stationery.
steak
juicy steak
steal
Steal money.
steel
iron and steel
stopped
straight
straight as an arrow
strait
sail through the strait
sugar
suite
hotel suite
sum
sum of money

summer
sun
sun and moon
Sunday
suppose
sure
surprise
sweet
sweet candy
swimming

T **tail**
dog's tail
tale
tale of woe
teacher
tear
than
Thanksgiving
the
their
their book
them
then
there
There it is.
they
they're
They're ready.
things
though
thought
threw
threw the ball
throne
king's throne
through
through the tunnel
thrown
has thrown the ball
tide
high tide
time
tired
to
Go to the store.
today
toe
toe of the foot
together
tonight
too
Too bad!
tow
Tow the car.
tried

trouble
truly
Tuesday
two
one, two, three

U undo
Undo the wrong.
undue
undue strife
until
urn
coffee urn
used
usually

V vain
tried in vain
vane
weather vane
veil
veil on a hat
vein
vein and artery
very

W wail
baby's wail
waist
around the waist
wait
Wait for me!
want
wanted
wares
sold his wares
warn
warn of danger
was
waste
Haste makes waste.
way
one way

we
We are here.
weak
The sound is weak.
wear
Wear this dress.
weather
The weather is hot.
weave
Weave the cloth.
Wednesday

wee
wee baby
week
end of the week
weigh
They weigh 5 pounds.
weight
Her weight is 50 pounds.
we'll
We'll see.
went

were

we've
We've had fun.
whale
whale in the sea
wheel
car's wheel
when

where
Where are you?
whether
whether or not
which
Which one is yours?
whine
dog's whine
whole
the whole thing

wholly
wholly useless
whose
Whose is it?
will
wine
Drink the wine.
witch
wicked witch
with
woman
women
won
He won first prize.
won't
wood
Chop wood.
wore
He wore a hat.
worn
an old worn coat
would
He would know.
wrap
Wrap a package.
wring
Wring out the clothes.
write
Write a letter.
writing
written
wrote

Y yoke
yoke for the animals
yolk
yolk of an egg
you

your

you're
You're the winner.

When you are talking to a friend and that person stops in the middle of a sentence, you often know how your friend will finish the sentence. When you are reading a book and you come to the bottom of a page, you often know what the author will say at the top of the next page. In both cases, you are *predicting*, or thinking ahead. When you predict, you use your experience and your knowledge of language to think of what might come next.

The twenty Prediction lessons in this section of Language Clues will give you practice in predicting as you read. You will hear stories that are divided into five segments. After each of the first four segments, you will answer a question on what you think will happen next. Often, after the fifth and last segment, you will be asked a question on the whole story.

How to Do Prediction Lessons

Your teacher will read the story, stopping after each segment. While each segment is being read, concentrate on the ideas, not the words. Think about what is happening and what is likely to happen. After each of the first four segments, you will be asked to predict what will happen next. After the fifth and last segment, you will often be asked a question on the whole story.

You will write your answers on an answer sheet, not in this book. Your teacher will tell you how to set up your answer sheet. Your teacher will also help you check your answers.

PREDICTION

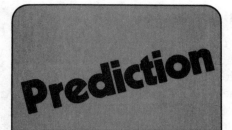

Prediction

DA 1

Cycle Words

actually	enemy
celebrate	familiar
command	flare
curiosity	instant
discovery	realize

Other Words

footprints	gunfire

DA 2

Cycle Words

agree	hesitate
argued	hobby
business	nephew
expert	particular
explanation	Tuesday

Proper Nouns

Leon	Tuesday
Stuart	

"The Lost Patrol" _____ DA 1

1. What did the captain find?

   a. Fresh footprints in the snow c. An enemy soldier
   b. An animal in a trap d. One of the rescue team, asleep

2. What will the captain order his men to do?

   a. Turn back!
   b. Be careful not to use strong language!
   c. Take cover and get ready in case of an attack!
   d. Use the radio to call for help!

3. What was the captain thinking?

   a. He knew that voice!
   b. They were being attacked!
   c. The rescue team was signaling him.
   d. He wished he'd written home more often.

4. What will happen next?

   a. The flare won't go off.
   b. The rescue team will find the lost men.
   c. The captain will be shot.
   d. The rescue team will attack the machine gun.

5. What was the main idea of the story?

   a. The captain loved a party.
   b. The missing men were glad to be found.
   c. The rescue team was glad to be found.
   d. The captain was willing to take a chance to save his men.

"The Ice Skater" _____ DA 2

1. What will the two boys do?

   a. Stay home c. Go ice skating
   b. Go to the movies d. Go fishing

2. What will Leon do?

   a. Continue to skate
   b. Stop skating
   c. Fall down
   d. Ask the others to skate with him

3. What will Stuart do?

   a. Go home
   b. Start a fight with Leon
   c. Try to skate like Leon
   d. Ask Leon to skate a while longer

4. What will Leon do?

   a. Try to help Stuart c. Tell Stuart to get off the ice
   b. Skate in his socks d. Fall down

5. Why did Leon fall down when he practiced?

   a. Leon was a bad skater.
   b. Leon always fell when other people were around.
   c. Leon didn't practice very much.
   d. Leon was still learning how to skate well.

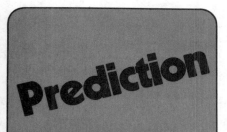

Prediction

DA 3

Cycle Words

avenue	paragraph
declare	person
experiment	September
natural	surface
nature	volcano

Proper Nouns

Barbara	June
English	

Other Word

uneven

DA 4

Cycle Words

acrobat	mystery
artist	obey
detective	private
hotel	seventh
magician	upset

1. What will Barbara's marks be like?

   a. All her marks will be good.
   b. All her marks will be bad.
   c. She will have some good marks and some bad marks.
   d. She will fail everything.

2. Where will Barbara go next?

   a. Home
   b. Back to school
   c. To the movies
   d. She will stay at the zoo.

3. What will Barbara do?

   a. Hide her marks
   b. Show her marks to her father
   c. Throw away her marks
   d. Say that she never got any marks

4. What will Barbara do after talking to her father?

   a. She'll do less work at school.
   b. She'll pretend to work harder at school.
   c. She'll drop out of school.
   d. She'll work harder at school.

5. Why did Barbara start to enjoy the other classes?

   a. She had new teachers.
   b. All her classes were about nature.
   c. She was finally learning something from them.
   d. She had made new friends in her classes.

1. What will the storyteller talk about next?

   a. Why her life is pretty quiet
   b. What happened when the show people stayed at the hotel
   c. How to become a hotel detective
   d. Private detectives

2. What could a bunch of bananas mean?

   a. The hotel detective liked to eat bananas.
   b. One of the hotel workers grew bananas.
   c. The hotel gave away free bananas.
   d. There was a monkey in the hotel.

3. Which two people is the detective thinking of?

   a. The acrobat and the magician
   b. The singer and the artist
   c. The artist and the private detective
   d. The young woman and the window cleaner

4. Who does the detective think took the necklace?

   a. The acrobat
   b. The magician
   c. The singer
   d. The monkey

5. Which of the following best tells what the story is about?

   a. An acrobat and a magician stay at a hotel.
   b. A hotel detective finds out that a monkey is a thief.
   c. A monkey hides in a hotel.
   d. A hotel detective slips on a banana skin.

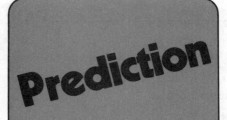

Prediction

DA 5

Cycle Words

August	damage
champion	demand
collect	immediately
collection	sixth
condition	twelfth

Proper Nouns

Arnie	Reggie Jackson
Harvey	Tim Foli
Jim Rooker	

DA 6

Cycle Words

figure	horrify
flicker	screech
ghost	shiver
gloomy	terror
groan	vanish

Other Word

grandparents

"The Collection" _____ DA 5

1. What will Harvey decide to do?

    a. Go to the baseball game
    b. Buy more baseball cards
    c. Save his money instead of spending it
    d. Go to the movies

2. Where will Harvey go?

    a. To the baseball game   c. To his home
    b. To the movies   d. To Arnie's house

3. What will Harvey do?

    a. Steal Arnie's card
    b. Leave Arnie's card where it is
    c. Tear up Arnie's card
    d. Ask Arnie for the card again

4. What will Arnie think happened to the card?

    a. He lost it.   c. He threw it away.
    b. Harvey took it.   d. His mother threw it away.

5. Why did Harvey give back the card?

    a. He was afraid Arnie would beat him up.
    b. He thought Arnie would tell his father.
    c. He realized that it was wrong to steal.
    d. He found another Jim Rooker.

"The Last Stop" _____ DA 6

1. What will the storyteller do?

    a. Look out of the window   c. Get something to eat
    b. Go back to sleep   d. Go to work

2. What will the storyteller realize?

    a. The driver is a friend of hers.
    b. There are no passengers on the bus.
    c. The bus is full of ghosts.
    d. The bus is stuck.

3. How does the storyteller feel when she hears the bus driver's words?

    a. Happy   c. Sleepy
    b. Frightened   d. Sad

4. Why is the storyteller "frozen to the spot"?

    a. She is afraid of riding on buses.
    b. The driver is not dressed right.
    c. There are no passengers on the bus.
    d. She recognizes the driver of the ghost bus.

5. Why did the ghost bus visit the storyteller?

    a. To scare her
    b. To warn her not to get on the bus
    c. To tell her to become a bus driver
    d. To keep her from getting to work

Prediction

DA 7

Cycle Words

ache	eyelid
examination	health
examine	medicine
eyebrow	nurse
eyelash	pain

Proper Nouns

Dr. Fred Madison

Dr. Michael Jackson

Rhoda Harris

DA 8

Cycle Words

brass	music
flute	musician
guitar	pause
instrument	perform
lip	trumpet

Proper Noun

Harry

Other Words

backstage   onstage

"Something in Her Eye" _____ DA 7

1. What will Rhoda do?

   a. Go home   c. Rub her eye again
   b. See the doctor   d. Keep walking down the street

2. What will happen?

   a. The doctor will examine Rhoda's eye.
   b. The doctor will go home.
   c. Rhoda will get an earache.
   d. The doctor will not want to examine Rhoda's eye.

3. How will Rhoda feel?

   a. Angry that she can't get help
   b. Happy that she doesn't need medicine for her ear
   c. Afraid that the doctor will hurt her
   d. Sad for the doctor

4. How will the patient help Rhoda?

   a. He will take her home.
   b. He will take her to another ear, nose, and throat doctor.
   c. He will tell her how to get something out of her eye.
   d. He will help her find a job.

5. What kind of story is this?

   a. Funny   c. Serious
   b. Sad   d. Fairy tale

"The Trumpet Player" _____ DA 8

1. What is Harry going to do?

   a. Keep practicing   c. Stay home
   b. Leave for the hall d. Go to the movies

2. What will Harry do about the flat tire?

   a. Wait for another driver to help him
   b. Walk to a garage
   c. Walk to the hall
   d. Change the tire

3. What will the police do?

   a. Give Harry a speeding ticket
   b. Put Harry in jail
   c. Drive Harry to the hall in their car
   d. Make Harry take a driver's test

4. What will Harry do now?

   a. Borrow someone else's trumpet
   b. Go back for his trumpet
   c. Go home
   d. Stay backstage and listen to the music

5. What kind of story is this meant to be?

   a. Scary   c. Funny
   b. Serious   d. True

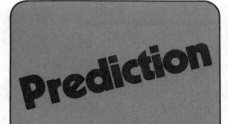

Prediction

DA 9

Cycle Words

burst	flood
December	news
earthquake	newspaper
enormous	shelter
explode	siren

Proper Nouns

California	Susan

DA 10

Cycle Words

astronaut	platform
flight	protection
million	rocket
orbit	soar
planet	telescope

Proper Nouns

Earth	Mars

Other Word

nowhere

"The Earthquake" _____ **DA 9**

1. What would happen after the dogs began to bark?

   a. Their masters would feed them.
   b. Their masters would take them out for a walk.
   c. An earthquake would begin.
   d. Susan would complain to the dogs' masters.

2. What would happen if the pipes kept bending?

   a. They would stick out of the wall.
   b. They would break and shoot water all over the house.
   c. They would bend back into place.
   d. Susan would have to live with bent pipes.

3. What would Susan do after the earthquake stopped?

   a. See if her house was badly damaged
   b. Leave the place immediately
   c. Go to a neighbor's house for breakfast
   d. Buy a new house

4. What would Susan do when she heard the sirens?

   a. Wait for the police who were coming to help
   b. Go to a shelter
   c. Hold her hands over her ears
   d. Hide from the police

5. Why did Susan laugh?

   a. She looked funny.
   b. She remembered a joke.
   c. The television people were funny.
   d. It was silly to be angry about not being on television.

"A Success" _____ **DA 10**

1. What will the astronaut do next?

   a. Repair the rocket   c. Step off the platform
   b. Get into the rocket   d. Destroy the rocket

2. What job is he going to perform?

   a. Fly the rocket to Mars   c. Fly the rocket to Earth
   b. Repair the rocket   d. Destroy the rocket

3. What will he do after the ship finishes orbiting Mars?

   a. Return to Earth   c. Wait for orders from Earth
   b. Land on Mars   d. Land on Earth

4. What does the astronaut plan to do now?

   a. Stay on Mars until he finds life
   b. Wait for orders from Earth
   c. Fly back to Mars
   d. Fly back to Earth

5. Why is this story called "A Success"?

   a. The astronaut found life on Mars.
   b. The astronaut found life on Earth.
   c. The astronaut performed his job well.
   d. The astronaut was able to fly back to Earth.

Prediction

DA 11

Cycle Words

buck	rodeo
corral	rough
disgrace	saddle
gallop	stallion
mare	tame

Proper Nouns

Lillie   Tex

Sam

Other Word

cowboy

DA 12

Cycle Words

equal	stolen
freedom	surrender
jailer	suspect
prisoner	threaten
quarrel	waist

Proper Nouns

Darryl   Sophie

Mr. Brown

Other Word

countless

"Sam" _____ DA 11

1. What will happen next?

    a. Tex won't come to the rodeo.
    b. Tex and Sam will meet at the rodeo.
    c. Sam won't show up at the rodeo.
    d. There will be no rodeo this year.

2. Who will Lillie say the "bag of bones" is?

    a. Sam   c. Tex
    b. Her brother   d. Herself

3. What will happen next?

    a. Lillie will hit Tex for laughing at Sam.
    b. Lillie will become the next rodeo champion.
    c. Sam will remember where he had met Tex before.
    d. Sam will kick Tex for laughing at him.

4. What will happen next?

    a. Sam will think of a way to beat Tex.
    b. Sam will pull out of the contest.
    c. Sam will lose again to Tex.
    d. Tex will pull out of the contest.

5. How did Sam feel when Tex fell off?

    a. Sad   c. Delighted
    b. Afraid   d. Bored

"Sophie's Fortune" _____ DA 12

1. What will Sophie's father say?

    a. Darryl is too old to marry Sophie.
    b. Sophie hasn't known Darryl long enough to marry him.
    c. Darryl only wants Sophie for her money.
    d. Sophie is too old to marry Darryl.

2. What will Sophie find out about Darryl?

    a. He has deserted her.   c. He doesn't own a watch.
    b. He has lost her address.   d. He found a better job.

3. What will Sophie do next?

    a. Go out and search for Darryl
    b. Marry Darryl's best friend
    c. Go on waiting for Darryl
    d. Open up a store

4. Who is coming to visit Sophie?

    a. Her father's ghost   c. Her husband
    b. Her old school teacher   d. Darryl

5. What have you learned about Sophie?

    a. Once she fell in love, she loved forever.
    b. She had wanted to get even with Darryl for a long time.
    c. She liked to sit by the window and watch the people walk by.
    d. She was afraid to go outside.

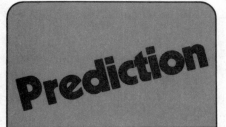

Prediction

DA 13

Cycle Words

action	dull
actor	fort
bullet	magazine
cast	movie
character	western

Other Words

gunfight   tryout

DA 14

Cycle Words

colonel	salute
cot	soldier
jeep	supplies
medal	supply
officer	uniform
rifle	

Proper Noun

Alan

Other Word

gunfire

"The Actor" _____ DA 13

1. What will the actor do?

   a. Try out for a part in the movie
   b. Throw away the magazine
   c. Cast his own western movie
   d. Go to sleep

2. What will happen next in the movie?

   a. The mean character will tell the star how to get to the fort.
   b. The star will give up trying to find the fort.
   c. There will be a gunfight.
   d. The mean character will talk to the star some more.

3. What will the actor think?

   a. The man wants his part.   c. He lost the part.
   b. The man is mean.   d. This is his tryout.

4. What will the actor do?

   a. Tell the man where the fort is
   b. Say his line from the movie
   c. Walk away from the man
   d. Tell the man to go away

5. What kind of story is this?

   a. Serious   c. Sad
   b. Amusing   d. Frightening

"A Hero" _____ DA 14

1. What will Alan do?

   a. Run back to the fighting
   b. Hide until he finds out who is calling
   c. Keep on running down the road
   d. Run right over to the person who needs help

2. Who was calling for help?

   a. The driver of the jeep   c. Nobody
   b. The supply officer   d. An enemy

3. What will Alan do?

   a. Run away
   b. Kill the driver
   c. Help the driver
   d. Give himself up to the enemy

4. How will Alan seem to the people back at camp?

   a. Afraid   c. Shy
   b. Stupid   d. Brave

5. Why did Alan save the driver and bring back the supplies?

   a. He needed the supplies to run away.
   b. The driver was his father.
   c. He wanted people to call him a hero.
   d. His need to help the driver and the soldiers back at camp was greater than his fear.

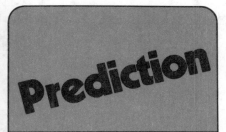

Prediction

DA 15

Cycle Words

acre	heap
bushel	orchard
chore	pear
crop	scythe
harvest	wheelbarrow

Proper Nouns

Danny	Uncle Al

DA 16

Cycle Words

anchor	pirate
aye	seaport
cargo	tide
crew	voyage
mast	wharf

Proper Nouns

Anubis	Egyptian

Other Words

starless	unseen
unloading	

"A New Summer" _____ DA 15

1. What will Danny do after hearing about his Uncle Al's color television?

    a. Stay home
    b. Ask his parents to buy a color television
    c. Go to visit his Uncle Al
    d. Get a job to buy a color television

2. What will Danny decide to do?

    a. Help Al
    b. Refuse to help Al
    c. Ask to go back home
    d. Ask Al where the television is

3. What is Danny going to do with the wheelbarrow?

    a. Carry it to the fruit
    b. Carry the fruit in it
    c. Ask somebody how to use it
    d. Leave it where it is

4. How will Danny spend the rest of his vacation?

    a. Watching television
    b. Sitting at home
    c. Working with Al
    d. Learning to drive the truck

5. What did Danny learn this summer?

    a. How to use a wheelbarrow
    b. The importance of doing new things
    c. Watching television is more fun than farming
    d. Where to toss the bad fruit

"The Anubis" _____ DA 16

1. What will the storyteller do about the ship out in the bay?

    a. Call the police
    b. Try to sneak aboard
    c. Ask the ship's captain for a job
    d. Ask to have the ship moved closer to shore

2. What will happen next?

    a. The ship's crew will catch the storyteller.
    b. The police will catch the storyteller.
    c. The storyteller will find a hiding place on the ship.
    d. The storyteller will ask the crew for dry clothes.

3. What will happen next?

    a. The storyteller will go back on deck.
    b. The storyteller will stay hidden.
    c. The storyteller will jump overboard and swim back to shore.
    d. The storyteller will be discovered.

4. What will the storyteller find on deck?

    a. A pirate crew
    b. The ship's captain
    c. No one
    d. The crew, asleep

5. What is the author's message?

    a. Never sneak aboard a ship.
    b. Sea storms are dangerous.
    c. Sailors are strange people.
    d. Killers cannot escape being punished.

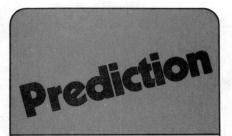

Prediction

DA 17

Cycle Words

blizzard	polar
Eskimo	reindeer
hunger	seal
icy	surround
northern	temperature

Other Words

alongside	unknown
firewood	

DA 18

Cycle Words

anger	stalk
battle	swamp
companion	tiger
hut	tropical
jungle	warrior

Other Words

sundown	useless
sunup	

1. What will the storyteller do?

   a. Buy a gun to shoot the enemy
   b. Hide at a friend's house
   c. Build a shelter against the coming winter
   d. Go swimming with the seal

2. What will happen next?

   a. Snow will fall.
   b. The storyteller will move south.
   c. The cabin will fall apart.
   d. The storyteller will tame the reindeer.

3. What will the storyteller do?

   a. Die of hunger
   b. Go fishing
   c. Buy a warm winter coat
   d. Trade the fur for a car

4. What will happen next?

   a. A wolf will blow down the door.
   b. The storyteller will nail the door shut.
   c. The seal will bring in some fish.
   d. The storyteller will open the door.

5. What have you learned about the storyteller?

   a. The storyteller found peace.
   b. The storyteller is an Eskimo.
   c. The storyteller is hunting for gold.
   d. The storyteller is an escaped prisoner.

"The Killer" _____ DA 18

1. What will the storyteller do with the gun?

   a. Throw it away
   b. Sell it
   c. Hunt for the tiger with it
   d. Kill himself

2. Where will the storyteller go?

   a. On into the jungle after the tiger
   b. Home to wait for the tiger to come to him
   c. Into the swamp to kill another tiger
   d. On a vacation

3. What will the storyteller do?

   a. Hide in his hut
   b. Ask his brother to help the boy
   c. Tell the boy to go away
   d. Try to help the boy

4. What will the storyteller do about the tiger?

   a. Kill the tiger
   b. Run away from the tiger
   c. Give his gun to the boy and tell him to kill the tiger
   d. Feed the tiger

5. What kind of man is the storyteller?

   a. One who pleases only himself
   b. One who puts his life in danger for no good reason
   c. One who finds courage because of his need to help others
   d. One who finds fun in killing

Prediction

DA 19

Cycle Words

beak	mutter
disturb	parrot
flutter	swan
geese	swoop
grumble	woodpecker

Proper Nouns

Egypt	Phoenix
Greece	Prometheus
Greek	

DA 20

Cycle Words

burro	lonesome
canyon	mesa
coyote	pioneer
frontier	prairie
howl	settler

Proper Nouns

Great Spirit	Sykes
Indians	

Other Word

faraway

"Prometheus and the Phoenix"_____ DA 19

1. What will the storyteller say about Prometheus?

   a. Prometheus discovered fire.
   b. Prometheus wasn't really a Greek.
   c. Prometheus did not give people the gift of fire.
   d. Prometheus lived for thousands of years.

2. When will Prometheus first see fire?

   a. On his birthday
   b. The following year
   c. The day he catches a parrot
   d. On one of the Phoenix's rebirth days

3. What will happen next?

   a. The Phoenix will help Prometheus become famous.
   b. The Phoenix will tell Prometheus an even sadder story.
   c. The Phoenix will tell Prometheus to fly south.
   d. The Phoenix will send Prometheus to a hospital for disturbed people.

4. What will Prometheus do?

   a. Run away from the crazy bird
   b. Help the Phoenix build a nest
   c. Go to Egypt and study magic
   d. Catch the Phoenix and sell it as a talking bird

5. After reading this story you know that

   a. the story is true.   c. birds can write as well as talk.
   b. Prometheus drowned in the lake. d. the story is make-believe.

"The Treasure"_____ DA 20

1. What did the Indians do in the desert?

   a. Wait for it to rain
   b. Trade with unfriendly tribes
   c. Stay there until they died
   d. Make bows and arrows

2. What is Sykes going to do?

   a. Listen to more stories
   b. Dream about the treasure
   c. Go into the desert to find the treasure
   d. Stay out of the desert

3. What does Sykes plan to do in the canyon?

   a. Look for the treasure   c. Rest
   b. Look for food and water   d. Hide a treasure

4. Where will Sykes look for the treasure?

   a. In the Indian remains   c. In another canyon
   b. At the mesa   d. In town

5. Why was water the treasure?

   a. In the desert, water was more important than gold.
   b. Water was all the Indians had.
   c. The Indians used water to buy things.
   d. The Indians always kept water in the ground.

DA 1

WORDS IN SENTENCES

1. realize
2. battery
3. fact
4. command
5. instant
6. enemy
7. accident
8. flare
9. ancestor
10. celebrate
11. beef
12. convenient
13. frozen
14. purpose
15. familiar
16. information
17. curiosity
18. envelope
19. discovery
20. actually

WORD PLAY

A

21. enemy
22. accident
23. discovery
24. curiosity
25. celebrate
26. ancestor
27. command
28. fact
29. purpose
30. information

B

31. frozen
32. instant
33. flare
34. realize
35. convenient
36. familiar
37. beef
38. actually
39. envelope
40. battery

WORDS IN STORIES

A

41. information
42. battery
43. enemy
44. command
45. flare

B

46. purpose
47. frozen
48. beef
49. instant
50. fact

C

51. accident
52. convenient
53. ancestor
54. familiar
55. realize

D

56. envelope
57. actually
58. curiosity
59. discovery
60. celebrate

DA 2

WORDS IN SENTENCES

1. patient
2. yesterday
3. opposite
4. explanation
5. argue
6. general
7. death
8. government
9. particular
10. impatient
11. nephew
12. married
13. hesitate
14. business
15. expert
16. Tuesday
17. hobby
18. habit
19. agree
20. possession

WORD PLAY

A

21. general
22. patient
23. Tuesday
24. nephew
25. possession

B

26. argue
27. habit
28. government
29. opposite
30. business

C

31. particular
32. explanation
33. expert
34. impatient
35. married
36. hobby
37. hesitate
38. death
39. agree
40. yesterday

WORDS IN STORIES

A
41. habit
42. hobby
43. agree
44. death
45. hesitate

B
46. government
47. general
48. particular
49. opposite
50. patient

C
51. Tuesday
52. business
53. explanation
54. expert
55. argue

D
56. yesterday
57. married
58. possession
59. impatient
60. nephew

DA 3

WORDS IN SENTENCES
1. shark
2. dangerous
3. experiment
4. nature
5. scientist
6. declare
7. appearance
8. alligator
9. crocodile
10. support
11. surface
12. level
13. avenue
14. September
15. natural
16. volcano
17. cub
18. shift
19. person
20. paragraph

WORD PLAY

A
21. volcano
22. cub
23. alligator
24. crocodile
25. person
26. nature
27. scientist
28. experiment
29. avenue
30. shark

B
31. appearance
32. level
33. dangerous
34. support
35. September
36. surface
37. shift
38. natural
39. paragraph
40. declare

WORDS IN STORIES

A
41. scientist
42. shark
43. paragraph
44. support
45. experiment

B
46. alligator
47. crocodile
48. appearance
49. declare
50. dangerous

C
51. shift
52. level
53. surface
54. September
55. volcano

D
56. natural
57. cub
58. person
59. avenue
60. nature

DA 4

WORDS IN SENTENCES
1. perfect
2. artist
3. hotel
4. distance
5. committee
6. mystery
7. upset
8. admit
9. acrobat
10. popular
11. admire
12. magician
13. control
14. private
15. seventeen
16. mysterious
17. seventh
18. detective
19. obey
20. national

WORD PLAY

A
21. control
22. seventeen
23. obey
24. admit
25. admire
26. committee
27. seventh
28. artist
29. mystery
30. acrobat
31. distance
32. magician
33. hotel
34. detective

B
35. national
36. mysterious
37. perfect
38. upset
39. private
40. popular

WORDS IN STORIES

A

41. detective
42. distance
43. obey
44. mysterious
45. private

B

46. magician
47. seventh
48. mystery
49. popular
50. acrobat

C

51. admit
52. hotel
53. perfect
54. upset
55. control

D

56. seventeen
57. committee
58. artist
59. national
60. admire

DA 5

WORDS IN SENTENCES

1. demand
2. damage
3. collection
4. victory
5. imitate
6. champion
7. August
8. condition
9. defend
10. strength
11. collect
12. twelfth
13. invent
14. avoid
15. immediately
16. rise
17. sixth
18. invention
19. program
20. develop

WORD PLAY

A

21. rise
22. avoid
23. immediately
24. champion
25. invent
26. demand
27. collect
28. condition
29. invention
30. imitate

B

31. twelfth
32. victory
33. strength
34. program
35. August
36. collection
37. sixth
38. damage
39. develop
40. defend

WORDS IN STORIES

A

41. rise
42. demand
43. condition
44. strength
45. champion

B

46. invent
47. sixth
48. imitate
49. develop
50. invention

C

51. August
52. collect
53. immediately
54. collection
55. program

D

56. twelfth
57. defend
58. damage
59. avoid
60. victory

REVIEW LESSON DA 1-5

A

1. mysterious
4. committee
6. Tuesday
8. alligator
10. crocodile
11. fact
14. scientist
15. information
18. twelfth
19. demand
22. government
24. impatient
25. ancestors
28. agree
30. declare
31. national
34. obey

B

36. admit
38. appearance
39. convenient
42. invent
44. familiar
46. purpose
47. experiment
50. battery
51. develop
54. seventeen
56. surface
58. volcano
60. flare
61. business
64. imitate
66. invention

C

68. acrobat
70. sixth
71. nephew
74. dangerous
75. champion
78. death
79. rise
82. distance
83. perfect
86. shift
87. instant
90. hesitate
91. level
93. support
96. accident
98. condition
99. natural

DA 6

WORDS IN SENTENCES

1. yell
2. silence
3. ghost
4. thankful
5. peace
6. creature
7. dreadful
8. horrify
9. cheerful
10. flicker
11. gloomy
12. fortunate
13. peaceful
14. terror
15. groan
16. shiver
17. dozen
18. screech
19. figure
20. vanish

WORD PLAY

A

21. fortunate
22. gloomy
23. yell
24. terror
25. ghost
26. peace
27. figure
28. creature
29. dozen
30. silence

B

31. dreadful
32. peaceful
33. thankful
34. cheerful

C

35. flicker
36. shiver
37. screech
38. groan
39. vanish
40. horrify

WORDS IN STORIES

A

41. flicker
42. screech
43. vanish
44. yell
45. peace

B

46. peaceful
47. silence
48. creature
49. horrify
50. dreadful

C

51. fortunate
52. cheerful
53. dozen
54. thankful
55. gloomy

D

56. groan
57. terror
58. figure
59. ghost
60. shiver

DA 7

WORDS IN SENTENCES

1. eyebrow
2. doubt
3. nurse
4. pain
5. wound
6. examination
7. Wednesday
8. possibly
9. cure
10. disease
11. health
12. medicine
13. breathe
14. stomach
15. length
16. eyelash
17. ache
18. poison
19. eyelid
20. examine

WORD PLAY

A

21. ache
22. wound
23. examine
24. doubt
25. disease

B

26. medicine
27. health
28. eyelash
29. length
30. pain
31. eyebrow

C

32. cure
33. possibly
34. breathe
35. eyelid
36. Wednesday
37. examination
38. poison
39. stomach
40. nurse

WORDS IN STORIES

A

41. examination
42. nurse
43. eyelid
44. pain
45. cure

B

46. eyebrow
47. breathe
48. doubt
49. poison
50. wound

C

51. ache
52. health
53. disease
54. length
55. medicine

D

56. examine
57. eyelash
58. possibly
59. Wednesday
60. stomach

DA 8

WORDS IN SENTENCES

1. arrangement
2. grade
3. improvement
4. area
5. flute
6. music
7. professor
8. musician
9. pupil
10. guitar
11. instrument
12. perform
13. trumpet
14. lip
15. brass
16. praise
17. department
18. pause
19. score
20. improve

WORD PLAY

A

21. instrument
22. brass
23. trumpet
24. pause
25. music
26. score
27. flute
28. department
29. improvement
30. guitar

B

31. improve
32. arrangement
33. musician
34. lip
35. area
36. grade
37. perform
38. praise
39. pupil
40. professor

WORDS IN STORIES

A

41. score
42. arrangement
43. guitar
44. praise
45. improvement

B

46. brass
47. trumpet
48. improve
49. lip
50. perform

C

51. music
52. instrument
53. musician
54. pause
55. area

D

56. Department
57. Professor
58. flute
59. pupil
60. grade

WORDS IN SENTENCES

1. engineer
2. flood
3. report
4. news
5. shelter
6. December
7. earthquake
8. noon
9. newspaper
10. enormous
11. explode
12. regular
13. midnight
14. necessary
15. customer
16. final
17. thrifty
18. ordinary
19. siren
20. burst

WORD PLAY

A

21. midnight
22. news
23. noon
24. newspaper
25. earthquake
26. shelter
27. burst
28. thrifty

B

29. explode
30. enormous
31. necessary
32. regular
33. final
34. flood
35. ordinary
36. report

C

37. siren
38. December
39. engineer
40. customer

A

41. earthquake
42. burst
43. flood
44. explode
45. enormous

B

46. final
47. noon
48. ordinary
49. siren
50. news

C

51. thrifty
52. customer
53. regular
54. December
55. midnight

D

56. necessary
57. shelter
58. newspaper
59. report
60. engineer

WORDS IN SENTENCES

1. astronaut
2. rocket
3. orbit
4. preparation
5. flight
6. telescope
7. platform
8. protection
9. suggest
10. modern
11. nineteen
12. interrupt
13. protect
14. zero
15. soar
16. ancient
17. ninth
18. planet
19. million
20. January

WORD PLAY

A

21. protection
22. interrupt
23. suggest
24. preparation

B

25. rocket
26. astronaut
27. platform
28. telescope
29. orbit
30. zero
31. million

C

32. protect
33. flight
34. January
35. soar
36. planet
37. ancient
38. modern
39. nineteen
40. ninth

A

41. preparation
42. astronaut
43. platform
44. telescope
45. million

B

46. planet
47. protection
48. flight
49. nineteen
50. orbit

C

51. interrupt
52. ninth
53. January
54. zero
55. modern

D

56. rocket
57. ancient
58. soar
59. suggest
60. protect

REVIEW LESSON DA 6-10

A

2. astronaut
3. report
6. ordinary
8. poison
9. disease
12. possibly
13. pain
16. flicker
18. screech
20. dreadful
22. horrify
23. vanish
25. telescope
28. instrument
29. ghost
32. examine
33. protection

B

36. eyelid
37. perform
39. music
42. preparation
44. doubt
46. grade
48. stomach
49. cheerful
52. guitar
53. pause
56. final
57. silence
59. newspaper
62. breathe
64. improvement
66. praise
68. thankful

C

70. Wednesday
71. regular
73. news
76. earthquake
77. flood
79. engineer
82. necessary
83. noon
86. protect
87. terror
89. nurse
92. wound
94. eyebrow
95. gloomy
98. million
100. burst

DA 11

WORDS IN SENTENCES

1. human
2. stallion
3. buck
4. steady
5. corral
6. hitch
7. insist
8. mare
9. gallop
10. difficult
11. rodeo
12. disgrace
13. rough
14. sleeve
15. pants
16. saddle
17. buckle
18. weary
19. stable
20. tame

WORD PLAY

A

21. rough
22. difficult
23. disgrace
24. tame
25. hitch
26. insist
27. steady
28. weary

B

29. saddle
30. corral
31. buck
32. stable
33. sleeve
34. buckle
35. stallion

C

36. rodeo
37. pants
38. mare
39. gallop
40. human

WORDS IN STORIES

A

41. rodeo
42. stallion
43. saddle
44. buck
45. buckle

B

46. tame
47. stable
48. insist
49. mare
50. gallop

C

51. weary
52. sleeve
53. hitch
54. pants
55. rough

D

56. human
57. difficult
58. corral
59. Steady
60. disgrace

WORDS IN SENTENCES

1. quarrel
2. shoulder
3. shove
4. jail
5. freedom
6. suspect
7. nervous
8. accuse
9. prisoner
10. fist
11. wrist
12. court
13. equal
14. arrest
15. stolen
16. prison
17. surrender
18. capture
19. waist
20. threaten

WORD PLAY

A

21. prison
22. arrest
23. shove
24. surrender
25. quarrel
26. nervous
27. equal

B

28. prisoner
29. fist
30. court
31. wrist
32. freedom
33. shoulder
34. jail
35. waist

C

36. capture
37. suspect
38. threaten
39. accuse
40. stolen

A

41. court
42. prison
43. stolen
44. nervous
45. accuse

B

46. equal
47. quarrel
48. shove
49. threaten
50. surrender

C

51. suspect
52. fist
53. shoulder
54. waist
55. arrest

D

56. prisoner
57. wrist
58. freedom
59. capture
60. jail

WORDS IN SENTENCES

1. movies
2. character
3. bullet
4. actor
5. cotton
6. western
7. fort
8. cast
9. slender
10. mustache
11. action
12. dull
13. wigwam
14. leather
15. material
16. magazine
17. punish
18. honest
19. rare
20. succeed

WORD PLAY

A

21. succeed
22. dull
23. action
24. honest
25. punish
26. slender
27. rare

B

28. character
29. fort
30. movies
31. mustache
32. magazine
33. western
34. cast
35. cotton

C

36. leather
37. wigwam
38. material
39. actor
40. bullet

A

41. magazine
42. cotton
43. leather
44. material
45. succeed

B

46. movies
47. cast
48. wigwam
49. fort
50. bullet

C

51. western
52. mustache
53. honest
54. action
55. punish

D

56. actor
57. character
58. slender
59. dull
60. rare

DA 14

WORDS IN SENTENCES

1. attention
2. salute
3. colonel
4. medal
5. rifle
6. position
7. soldier
8. uniform
9. motion
10. jeep
11. officer
12. quart
13. delivery
14. measure
15. amount
16. remind
17. supplies
18. eighteen
19. cot
20. eighth

WORD PLAY

A

21. supplies
22. officer
23. amount
24. position
25. eighth
26. uniform

B

27. motion
28. delivery
29. remind
30. eighteen
31. measure
32. quart

C

33. medal
34. cot
35. jeep
36. rifle
37. colonel
38. soldier
39. salute
40. attention

WORDS IN STORIES

A

41. delivery
42. cot
43. supplies
44. eighth
45. jeep

B

46. uniform
47. soldier
48. colonel
49. attention
50. salute

C

51. quart
52. measure
53. amount
54. remind
55. eighteen

D

56. rifle
57. position
58. motion
59. officer
60. medal

DA 15

WORDS IN SENTENCES

1. orchard
2. sour
3. pear
4. flavor
5. bushel
6. heap
7. harvest
8. October
9. scythe
10. acre
11. afford
12. expensive
13. wheelbarrow
14. future
15. quarter
16. crop
17. chore
18. weed
19. shepherd
20. responsible

WORD PLAY

A

21. responsible
22. future
23. sour
24. crop
25. expensive

B

26. orchard
27. October
28. acre
29. pear
30. shepherd
31. quarter
32. bushel
33. afford

C

34. harvest
35. heap
36. scythe
37. chore
38. flavor
39. wheelbarrow
40. weed

WORDS IN STORIES

A
41. chore
42. expensive
43. weed
44. acre
45. wheelbarrow

B
46. bushel
47. flavor
48. pear
49. heap
50. sour

C
51. October
52. orchard
53. crop
54. afford
55. harvest

D
56. shepherd
57. quarter
58. scythe
59. future
60. responsible

REVIEW LESSON DA 11-15

A
1. eighteen
4. remind
5. succeed
8. steady
9. October
11. harvest
14. slender
15. mustache
17. leather
20. waist
22. western
23. shoulder
26. attention
27. movies
29. afford
32. expensive
34. future

B
36. soldier
37. prisoner
40. nervous
41. officer
44. prison
46. fist
47. freedom
50. eighth
52. supplies
53. jeep
56. rifle
58. stolen
59. capture
61. motion
64. bullet
66. rough
67. surrender

C
70. stable
71. hitch
74. delivery
76. stallion
77. dull
80. difficult
81. weary
84. insist
85. crop
88. disgrace
89. punish
91. court
93. quart
95. bushel
98. action
99. responsible

DA 16

WORDS IN SENTENCES
1. neighborhood
2. wharf
3. seaport
4. landlord
5. suitcase
6. cargo
7. voyage
8. pirate
9. royal
10. eastern
11. navy
12. crew
13. mast
14. bare
15. tide
16. oar
17. shallow
18. Aye
19. anchor
20. stern

WORD PLAY

A
21. aye
22. eastern
23. stern
24. bare
25. royal
26. shallow

B
27. neighborhood
28. suitcase
29. seaport
30. landlord

C
31. crew
32. navy
33. anchor
34. tide
35. oar
36. mast
37. cargo
38. pirate
39. voyage
40. wharf

WORDS IN STORIES

A
41. eastern
42. tide
43. anchor
44. stern
45. voyage

B
46. navy
47. royal
48. mast
49. Aye
50. pirate

C
51. suitcase
52. oar
53. shallow
54. wharf
55. bare

D
56. seaport
57. cargo
58. crew
59. neighborhood
60. landlord

DA 17

WORDS IN SENTENCES

1. reindeer
2. Eskimo
3. northern
4. seal
5. polar
6. walrus
7. icy
8. blubber
9. temperature
10. refrigerator
11. glow
12. furnace
13. hunger
14. awkward
15. zone
16. blizzard
17. gradually
18. paddle
19. kayak
20. surround

WORD PLAY

A

21. surround
22. zone
23. glow
24. awkward
25. gradually
26. paddle
27. blubber
28. seal

B

29. reindeer
30. temperature
31. blizzard
32. walrus
33. kayak
34. refrigerator

C

35. icy
36. Eskimo
37. furnace
38. polar
39. hunger
40. northern

WORDS IN STORIES

A

41. Eskimo
42. reindeer
43. walrus
44. blubber
45. hunger

B

46. awkward
47. polar
48. icy
49. kayak
50. paddle

C

51. glow
52. Northern
53. temperature
54. furnace
55. refrigerator

D

56. seal
57. blizzard
58. zone
59. surround
60. gradually

DA 18

WORDS IN SENTENCES

1. league
2. treaty
3. battle
4. warrior
5. spear
6. tropical
7. companion
8. swamp
9. friendship
10. hut
11. jungle
12. bamboo
13. tiger
14. stalk
15. guest
16. dignity
17. anger
18. hurricane
19. southern
20. equator

WORD PLAY

A

21. bamboo
22. anger
23. hut
24. jungle
25. tiger
26. hurricane
27. league

B

28. southern
29. swamp
30. tropical
31. equator
32. friendship
33. battle

C

34. spear
35. guest
36. warrior
37. companion
38. treaty
39. stalk
40. dignity

WORDS IN STORIES

A
41. battle
42. treaty
43. warrior
44. dignity
45. league

B
46. southern
47. equator
48. tropical
49. bamboo
50. hurricane

C
51. swamp
52. companion
53. friendship
54. guest
55. anger

D
56. tiger
57. jungle
58. stalk
59. hut
60. spear

WORDS IN SENTENCES
1. woodpecker
2. beak
3. mutter
4. parrot
5. grumble
6. pigeon
7. squeal
8. claw
9. robin
10. uneasy
11. swoop
12. swan
13. flutter
14. trim
15. squawk
16. flock
17. geese
18. giggle
19. gull
20. disturb

WORD PLAY

A
21. uneasy
22. giggle
23. disturb
24. trim
25. grumble
26. flock
27. beak
28. claw

B
29. flutter
30. squeal
31. squawk
32. swoop
33. mutter

C
34. pigeon
35. swan
36. gull
37. parrot
38. woodpecker
39. geese
40. robin

WORDS IN STORIES

A
41. woodpecker
42. beak
43. swan
44. flutter
45. robin

B
46. flock
47. geese
48. swoop
49. disturb
50. pigeon

C
51. parrot
52. trim
53. claw
54. mutter
55. squawk

D
56. giggle
57. grumble
58. squeal
59. gull
60. uneasy

WORDS IN SENTENCES
1. burro
2. canyon
3. pioneer
4. mesa
5. coyote
6. howl
7. ruin
8. prairie
9. lonesome
10. frontier
11. rustle
12. sheriff
13. messenger
14. firm
15. roam
16. partner
17. rude
18. savage
19. settler
20. carpenter

WORD PLAY

A
21. sheriff
22. carpenter
23. partner
24. mesa
25. settler
26. pioneer

B
27. howl
28. rustle
29. ruin
30. roam
31. lonesome
32. savage
33. rude
34. canyon

C
35. prairie
36. burro
37. coyote
38. firm
39. frontier
40. messenger

WORDS IN STORIES

A

41. frontier
42. messenger
43. sheriff
44. firm
45. savage

B

46. carpenter
47. rude
48. settler
49. prairie
50. lonesome

C

51. ruin
52. rustle
53. mesa
54. coyote
55. howl

D

56. partner
57. canyon
58. burro
59. roam
60. pioneer

REVIEW LESSON DA 16-20

A

2. companion
3. royal
6. frontier
7. canyon
10. coyote
12. pioneer
13. mutter
15. giggle
18. anger
20. dignity
22. savage
24. rustle
26. Eastern
27. partner
29. battle
31. firm
34. guest

B

36. neighborhood
38. geese
40. swan
42. paddle
43. lonesome
46. pigeon
48. robin
49. beak
51. furnace
53. grumble
55. landlord
58. rude
60. temperature
62. icy
64. suitcase
66. friendship

C

68. equator
70. hurricane
72. southern
74. swoop
75. ruin
77. tropical
79. gull
82. crew
84. anchor
86. glow
87. wharf
90. tide
92. seaport
93. uneasy
96. parrot
97. squawk
100. jungle

Spelling Recognition Tests

The spelling recognition tests that follow should be used before you begin the *Words-in-Stories* exercise.

Number your paper from 1 to 20. Choose the correct spelling for each word and write either the word or the letter for the correct word on your answer sheet. Use the Answer Key on pages 148 and 149 to check your work.

Spelling Recognition Test

Number your paper from 1 to 20. Find the word on each line that is spelled correctly and write the word or its letter on your paper.

	A	B	C	D
1.	batery	battery	battiry	batrey
2.	realise	relize	relise	realize
3.	fact	fack	facte	factt
4.	enemie	enemy	enimy	enemey
5.	enstant	instent	instunt	instant
6.	comand	command	cammand	camand
7.	accident	acident	akcident	acsident
8.	flaer	flere	flare	flarre
9.	celebraite	celebrait	celebrat	celebrate
10.	ancestor	ancester	ansestor	ancesstor
11.	frosen	frozan	frozen	frosan
12.	beaf	beef	bief	befe
13.	convienent	conveneint	convenient	convinient
14.	perpuse	purpos	perpose	purpose
15.	information	infermation	infurmation	inforrmation
16.	familier	familiar	familer	familar
17.	invelop	envilope	invelope	envelope
18.	curiusity	curiositie	curiosity	cureosity
19.	actually	aktually	actualy	aktuallie
20.	diskoverie	discovery	discoverey	diskovery

Spelling Recognition Test

Number your paper from 1 to 20. Find the word on each line that is spelled correctly and write the word or its letter on your paper.

	A	B	C	D
1.	pashunt	patient	paytient	paitient
2.	yisterday	yestirday	yesturday	yesterday
3.	opposite	oposite	oppusite	oppossite
4.	explenation	explanation	explanasion	explenasion
5.	argui	argu	argue	argeu
6.	general	genural	gineral	generale
7.	dethe	deathe	deth	death
8.	guvernment	govurnment	government	goverment
9.	partikular	particular	particuler	perticular
10.	impashunt	impaytient	inpaitient	impatient
11.	nephew	nefew	nephue	nefue
12.	maryed	marryed	married	maried
13.	hesitate	hesetate	hesitait	hesetait
14.	bussiness	business	busines	businiss
15.	expirte	experte	expirt	expert
16.	Teusday	Tuseday	Tuesday	Tusday
17.	hobby	hobbie	hoby	hobbey
18.	habet	habit	habite	habbit
19.	aggree	agrie	agre	agree
20.	posession	possession	possesion	pussession

Spelling Recognition Test

Number your paper from 1 to 20. Find the word on each line that is spelled correctly and write the word or its letter on your paper.

	A	B	C	D
1.	shark	sharck	sharc	sharek
2.	dangerus	dangurous	dangurus	dangerous
3.	experement	experiment	expiriment	expirement
4.	naiture	naytur	nachure	nature
5.	sceintist	scientest	scientist	sientist
6.	declair	declare	declaire	declere
7.	appearance	apeerance	apearance	appeerance
8.	aligater	alygator	alligator	allygater
9.	crocodial	crocodile	crokodile	crokodial
10.	suport	supoart	supportt	support
11.	surface	serface	serfase	surphace
12.	levell	leval	level	levol
13.	avenew	avanue	avnanew	avenue
14.	September	Septembor	Setember	Septembore
15.	naturel	natural	nachurel	naturale
16.	volcaino	volcanoe	volcano	volkano
17.	cub	kub	cubb	kubb
18.	sheft	shiftt	schift	shift
19.	purson	persen	person	pursen
20.	paragraf	paragraph	parragraph	paregraph

Spelling Recognition Test

Number your paper from 1 to 20. Find the word on each line that is spelled correctly and write the word or its letter on your paper.

	A	B	C	D
1.	purfect	perfectt	purfeck	perfect
2.	artest	artist	artiste	aretist
3.	hotel	hotele	hotell	hotelle
4.	distence	destance	distanc	distance
5.	committee	committe	comittee	commitee
6.	mistery	mysterie	mystery	misterey
7.	upsett	upset	upsete	upsit
8.	admitt	admet	admit	addmit
9.	acrobat	ackrobat	akrobat	acrobate
10.	populair	populare	populer	popular
11.	admier	admire	admeir	addmire
12.	majisian	magecian	magician	mejician
13.	control	controle	controll	kontrol
14.	preyevate	privait	privut	private
15.	sevinteen	seventene	seventeen	siventeen
16.	mysterious	misterious	mystereous	mistereous
17.	siventh	sevinth	sevunth	seventh
18.	detecktive	detective	detektive	detecteve
19.	obey	obay	obbey	obaye
20.	nashional	nasional	national	nationale

Spelling Recognition Test

Number your paper from 1 to 20. Find the word on each line that is spelled correctly and write the word or its letter on your paper.

	A	B	C	D
1.	damand	demmand	demand	dammand
2.	damage	damaje	damege	dameje
3.	colection	collecshion	colecshion	collection
4.	victery	victory	vicktory	victury
5.	emitate	immitate	imitate	imitaite
6.	champeon	champiun	chammpion	champion
7.	August	Awgust	Augast	Awgast
8.	condicion	condition	condetion	cundition
9.	defend	deffend	difend	defind
10.	straingth	strenth	strength	stringth
11.	colect	collect	colleck	collectt
12.	twelth	twelveth	twilfth	twelfth
13.	envent	invent	envint	inventt
14.	avoid	avoide	aviod	avoidd
15.	emmediately	immidiately	immediately	immediatly
16.	reyes	wrise	risse	rise
17.	sexth	sixth	siksth	sixthe
18.	invintion	envention	invenshion	invention
19.	program	programm	programe	progrum
20.	divelop	develope	develop	devellop

Spelling Recognition Test

Number your paper from 1 to 20. Find the word on each line that is spelled correctly and write the word or its letter on your paper.

	A	B	C	D
1.	yelle	yell	yel	yele
2.	silance	silunce	sillence	silence
3.	ghost	gost	ghoste	goste
4.	thankfule	thankfel	thankful	thainkful
5.	peace	pease	pese	pece
6.	krecher	creture	creature	kreture
7.	dredful	dreadful	dreadfulle	dredfull
8.	horify	horrefy	horrefi	horrify
9.	cheerful	chierful	chearful	cherful
10.	fliker	flickur	flicker	flikur
11.	gluemy	gloomy	glumy	glume
12.	forchunate	forchewnate	fortunet	fortunate
13.	peaseful	peseful	peaceful	peceful
14.	terrer	terror	terorr	teror
15.	groan	grone	gron	groane
16.	shever	shiver	shivir	shevir
17.	dozun	dozin	duzen	dozen
18.	skreech	screeche	screech	skreeche
19.	figure	figyer	figyour	figyure
20.	vannish	vanish	vanishe	vanesh

Number your paper from 1 to 20. Find the word on each line that is spelled correctly and write the word or its letter on your paper.

	A	B	C	D
1.	eyebrow	eyebrau	ibrow	ibrau
2.	doubte	daut	dowt	doubt
3.	nerse	nurse	ners	nurce
4.	payn	pain	paine	payne
5.	wund	woond	wound	wunde
6.	eksamination	examenation	examinashion	examination
7.	Wednesday	Wenesday	Wenzday	Wednasday
8.	possiblie	posibly	possibly	possebly
9.	kure	cure	kyure	cyure
10.	dizease	desease	dizese	disease
11.	health	helth	hellth	healthe
12.	medecine	medisine	medicine	medesin
13.	breth	breathe	brethe	breeth
14.	stomach	stomack	stumach	stumack
15.	lenth	lingth	linth	length
16.	eyelashe	eyelash	ilash	ilashe
17.	acke	ak	ache	ake
18.	poison	poyson	poizon	poyzon
19.	eyelide	ilid	eyelid	ilide
20.	examin	eksamine	examan	examine

Spelling Recognition Test

Number your paper from 1 to 20. Find the word on each line that is spelled correctly and write the word or its letter on your paper.

	A	B	C	D
1.	arangement	arrangment	arrangemint	arrangement
2.	grade	graed	graid	gread
3.	improvment	improvement	improvemint	impruvement
4.	airea	arrea	area	arria
5.	floot	flute	flutte	floote
6.	music	mewsic	muzik	musik
7.	professer	proffesser	proffessor	professor
8.	muzishian	musishian	musician	muzician
9.	pupil	pewpil	pupel	puepil
10.	getar	guitare	getare	guitar
11.	enstrument	instrument	instrumint	enstrumint
12.	purform	perphorm	perform	performe
13.	trumpet	trumput	trummpet	trumpett
14.	lep	lipe	lipp	lip
15.	braze	brasse	brass	brase
16.	praise	prase	praize	praiz
17.	departmint	department	dipartment	dipartmint
18.	pawse	pauze	pause	pawze
19.	skore	scoer	skoer	score
20.	improve	emprove	impruve	empruve

Spelling Recognition Test

Number your paper from 1 to 20. Find the word on each line that is spelled correctly and write the word or its letter on your paper.

	A	B	C	D
1.	enginear	engineer	engeneer	ingeneer
2.	flud	flod	flode	flood
3.	report	repport	reportt	raport
4.	nuzs	news	newz	newes
5.	sheltor	shellter	shelter	sheltter
6.	December	Desember	Dicember	Decembor
7.	erthquake	earthkwake	erthkwake	earthquake
8.	nune	noone	noon	newn
9.	nuzspaper	newspaper	newzpaper	newspapor
10.	enormous	inormous	enormus	inormus
11.	eksplode	explod	eksplod	explode
12.	rigular	regulare	regular	reggular
13.	midnight	midnit	midnigt	midniht
14.	necesary	necessary	neccessary	neccesary
15.	kustomer	custermer	kustomor	customer
16.	finnal	finall	final	finail
17.	thrifty	threfty	thrifte	thriftie
18.	oredinary	ordenary	ordinarey	ordinary
19.	sirene	siren	sirin	sirein
20.	berst	burste	burst	burrst

Spelling Recognition Test

Number your paper from 1 to 20. Find the word on each line that is spelled correctly and write the word or its letter on your paper.

	A	B	C	D
1.	astrunaut	astronawt	astronaut	astranaut
2.	rockett	roket	rockit	rocket
3.	orbit	orebit	orbitt	orbet
4.	preperation	preparation	preparashun	preperashun
5.	flite	fligt	flight	fliht
6.	teleskope	teliscope	tileskope	telescope
7.	platforme	platform	platferm	plattform
8.	protection	protecktion	protecshun	protekshun
9.	sugest	suggeste	suggestt	suggest
10.	modurn	modern	moddern	modirn
11.	ninteen	nineteene	nineteen	nintean
12.	interrupt	enterrupt	interupt	interrup
13.	proteck	protict	protecte	protect
14.	zero	ziro	ziero	zeroe
15.	soare	soar	sor	soarr
16.	anceint	aincient	ancient	anshient
17.	nineth	nienth	neinth	ninth
18.	planet	planett	plannet	planut
19.	milion	mellion	million	milleon
20.	Januairy	January	Januwery	Januwhery

Spelling Recognition Test

Number your paper from 1 to 20. Find the word on each line that is spelled correctly and write the word or its letter on your paper.

A	B	C	D
1. human	humman	hewman	hueman
2. stalion	stallion	stalleon	staleon
3. buk	buc	buck	bucke
4. stedy	steaddy	steadie	steady
5. corrall	corral	correl	corrale
6. hich	hetch	hitch	hitche
7. insist	ensist	insyst	incist
8. mair	maire	maer	mare
9. galop	galope	gallop	gallope
10. difficult	dificult	diffikult	difficultt
11. rodio	rodeo	roedeo	rowdeo
12. desgrace	disgrac	disgrace	disgrase
13. ruf	ruff	rouf	rough
14. sleeve	sleve	sleev	sleave
15. panz	pants	pannts	pantts
16. saddel	sadle	saddal	saddle
17. bukle	buckel	buckle	bucle
18. weary	weery	wearey	wiery
19. stabel	stable	stayble	stabell
20. taim	taime	tamme	tame

Spelling Recognition Test

Number your paper from 1 to 20. Find the word on each line that is spelled correctly and write the word or its letter on your paper.

	A	B	C	D
1.	quarel	quarrele	quarell	quarrel
2.	sholder	shoulder	shouldor	sholdor
3.	shove	shuve	shov	shuv
4.	jale	jaile	jail	jaille
5.	fredom	freedom	freedome	freedum
6.	suspeck	suspict	suspect	suspick
7.	nervus	nervos	nervas	nervous
8.	accuse	ackuse	accews	acuse
9.	presoner	prizoner	prizenor	prisoner
10.	fisst	fist	fiste	fistt
11.	rist	wriste	wrist	riste
12.	court	cort	kourt	kort
13.	equall	equale	equl	equal
14.	arrest	arest	arrestt	arreste
15.	stollen	stolen	stolin	stollin
16.	prizon	prizen	prison	prisen
17.	surender	surrendor	surendor	surrender
18.	kapture	capture	capchure	kapchure
19.	waist	waiste	wayst	wast
20.	threten	thretten	threaten	threatin

Spelling Recognition Test

Number your paper from 1 to 20. Find the word on each line that is spelled correctly and write the word or its letter on your paper.

	A	B	C	D
1.	moveys	movies	moovies	mooveys
2.	character	caracter	charactor	caractor
3.	bullit	bulett	bullett	bullet
4.	acter	acktor	actor	acttor
5.	cottin	cotten	cotton	coton
6.	westirn	western	westtern	westerne
7.	fort	fortt	foart	foret
8.	kaste	kast	castt	cast
9.	slendir	slender	slinder	slendor
10.	mustache	moustache	mustash	moustashe
11.	acktion	acshion	action	akshion
12.	dulle	dull	dul	duhl
13.	wigwamm	wegwam	wigwame	wigwam
14.	leather	lether	leathor	leathir
15.	matearial	matereal	material	matierial
16.	magazene	magazine	magezine	magazean
17.	punnish	punesh	punishe	punish
18.	honest	honist	honnest	honust
19.	raire	raere	rare	rarre
20.	suceed	succeed	succede	suckceed

Spelling Recognition Test

Number your paper from 1 to 20. Find the word on each line that is spelled correctly and write the word or its letter on your paper.

	A	B	C	D
1.	attenshion	atention	attention	attintion
2.	salute	saloot	salewt	salut
3.	kernell	colonil	kernil	colonel
4.	medale	medal	medel	medil
5.	rifel	rifal	rifle	rifl
6.	position	posishion	possition	posishun
7.	soleger	solejer	soljier	soldier
8.	uneform	uniform	unniform	uniforme
9.	moshion	moshin	motion	moetion
10.	jeep	jeap	jepe	jeip
11.	oficer	offecer	officir	officer
12.	quort	quart	quarte	quorte
13.	delivery	dilivery	delivary	delivry
14.	mesure	meashure	measure	meshure
15.	ahmount	amownt	amountt	amount
16.	rimind	remind	reminde	riminde
17.	supplies	suplies	supplys	supplis
18.	eightteen	ateteen	eighteen	eigteen
19.	kot	cot	cote	cott
20.	athe	eith	aythe	eighth

DA-15   Spelling Recognition Test

Number your paper from 1 to 20. Find the word on each line that is spelled correctly and write the word or its letter on your paper.

	A	B	C	D
1.	orchard	orcherd	orechard	orcharde
2.	sowr	soure	saur	sour
3.	pere	pear	peare	perr
4.	flaver	flavore	flavor	flavere
5.	bushle	bushal	bushell	bushel
6.	heep	heap	heape	heepe
7.	harvest	harvist	harevest	harvost
8.	Oktober	Ocktober	October	Octobir
9.	scythe	sithe	sighth	sythe
10.	aker	acer	accre	acre
11.	aford	afforde	afford	aforde
12.	exspensive	expensive	expinsive	exspinsiv
13.	wheelbarrow	wheelbarow	weelbarow	weelbarrow
14.	futere	fuchure	futer	future
15.	quater	quartor	quarter	quartir
16.	krop	crop	cropp	crope
17.	chore	choar	chor	choare
18.	wede	wead	weed	weede
19.	sheperd	shepherd	shephird	shepheard
20.	responsable	responzible	responseable	responsible

Spelling Recognition Test

Number your paper from 1 to 20. Find the word on each line that is spelled correctly and write the word or its letter on your paper.

	A	B	C	D
1.	naborhood	neighborhood	neiborhood	naberhood
2.	worf	warf	wharf	whorf
3.	seaport	seeport	seaporte	seeporte
4.	landlorde	land lord	lanlord	landlord
5.	sutecase	suitcase	sootcase	sewtcase
6.	kargo	cargoe	cargo	kargoe
7.	voyage	voyije	voyige	voyaje
8.	pirat	piret	pirrate	pirate
9.	royal	royall	royel	royell
10.	eestern	eastern	eastirn	estern
11.	navey	navi	navy	navee
12.	krew	crue	krue	crew
13.	mast	mastt	masst	maste
14.	baire	bere	bare	barre
15.	tid	tide	tyde	tidde
16.	oar	oare	oair	oarr
17.	shalow	shalloe	shaloe	shallow
18.	Ayi	Aye	Aey	Aeye
19.	ainchor	ankor	anchor	ankore
20.	stirn	stearn	sterne	stern

Spelling Recognition Test

Number your paper from 1 to 20. Find the word on each line that is spelled correctly and write the word or its letter on your paper.

	A	B	C	D
1.	raindeer	reindear	raindear	reindeer
2.	Eskemo	Eskimo	Eskemow	Eskimoe
3.	northurn	northerne	northern	norethern
4.	seal	seel	seale	seele
5.	poler	polar	pollar	polur
6.	wallrus	walros	walras	walrus
7.	icey	isey	icy	icie
8.	blubber	bluber	blubbor	blubar
9.	temperture	tempurature	temperature	tempurture
10.	refrigerater	refrigerator	refrigurator	refridgerator
11.	glow	glo	glowe	gloew
12.	fernace	firnace	furnase	furnace
13.	hunger	hungir	hungar	hunnger
14.	awkwid	awkward	awkwerd	awkwurd
15.	zoan	zon	zone	zoane
16.	blizzard	blizard	blizzerd	blizzurd
17.	gradualy	gradjely	gradjelly	gradually
18.	paddel	paddle	padle	paddal
19.	kyak	kayack	kayak	kyack
20.	suround	serround	sirround	surround

Spelling Recognition Test

Number your paper from 1 to 20. Find the word on each line that is spelled correctly and write the word or its letter on your paper.

	A	B	C	D
1.	leeg	leag	league	leegue
2.	treety	treatie	treetie	treaty
3.	battle	battel	battal	batle
4.	warreor	warrier	warrior	warior
5.	speer	spear	speare	speere
6.	tropicle	tropicel	tropicall	tropical
7.	companyon	companion	cumpanion	comepanion
8.	swump	swammp	swamp	swampe
9.	friendship	freindship	frendship	frendshipp
10.	hutt	hute	whut	hut
11.	jungle	jungel	jungal	jungell
12.	bambu	bamboo	bambo	bammboo
13.	tyger	tigir	tiger	tygor
14.	stawk	stalk	stalke	stawke
15.	gest	guestt	gueste	guest
16.	dignety	dignitty	dignity	dignitie
17.	anger	angor	angir	ainger
18.	huricane	hurricane	hurricain	huricaine
19.	suthern	southirn	suthirn	southern
20.	equator	ekwator	equater	ekwater

Spelling Recognition Test

Number your paper from 1 to 20. Find the word on each line that is spelled correctly and write the word or its letter on your paper.

	A	B	C	D
1.	wouldpecker	woodpeckir	wouldpeckor	woodpecker
2.	beek	beak	beake	beeke
3.	mutter	muttir	muttor	muttar
4.	parott	parrott	parrot	parot
5.	grumbel	grumbal	grumbell	grumble
6.	pidgeon	pigeon	pigion	pidgion
7.	squeal	skweel	squeale	skweal
8.	clawe	klaw	claw	klawe
9.	roben	robbin	robine	robin
10.	uneasy	uneesy	uneazie	uneasie
11.	swupe	swoop	swoope	swup
12.	swone	swane	swan	swon
13.	flutter	fluter	fluttir	flutir
14.	trimm	trem	trime	trim
15.	squawk	skwawk	squauk	skwauk
16.	flok	flocke	flock	floke
17.	geece	geese	gease	geace
18.	giggel	giggal	gigle	giggle
19.	gulle	gull	gul	gule
20.	disterb	distirb	disturb	disturbe

Spelling Recognition Test

Number your paper from 1 to 20. Find the word on each line that is spelled correctly and write the word or its letter on your paper.

	A	B	C	D
1.	buro	burroe	burro	burow
2.	canyon	kanyon	canyen	kanyen
3.	pionear	pionere	pionier	pioneer
4.	messa	mesa	misa	mesae
5.	kyote	cyote	coyote	kiote
6.	howel	howil	howll	howl
7.	rewn	ruin	ruein	roon
8.	prairie	prayrie	prarie	prairey
9.	lonsome	lonesum	lonesome	lonsum
10.	frontear	frontier	fronteer	frontire
11.	russle	russel	rustel	rustle
12.	sheriff	sherriff	sherrif	shireff
13.	messinger	missenger	messenger	mesenger
14.	furm	firm	ferm	firme
15.	roame	rom	roamm	roam
16.	partner	partnor	partnir	parner
17.	rood	roode	rude	rudde
18.	savaje	savage	savege	savige
19.	setler	settlir	settlor	settler
20.	carpenter	carpentir	carpinter	carpintir

ANSWER KEY Spelling Recognition Tests

DA-1

1. B	11. C
2. D	12. B
3. A	13. C
4. B	14. D
5. D	15. A
6. B	16. B
7. A	17. D
8. C	18. C
9. D	19. A
10. A	20. B

DA-2

1. B	11. A
2. D	12. C
3. A	13. A
4. B	14. B
5. C	15. D
6. A	16. C
7. D	17. A
8. C	18. B
9. B	19. D
10. D	20. B

DA-3

1. A	11. A
2. D	12. C
3. B	13. D
4. D	14. A
5. C	15. B
6. B	16. C
7. A	17. A
8. C	18. D
9. B	19. C
10. D	20. B

DA-4

1. D	11. B
2. B	12. C
3. A	13. A
4. D	14. D
5. A	15. C
6. C	16. A
7. B	17. D
8. C	18. B
9. A	19. A
10. D	20. C

DA-5

1. C	11. B
2. A	12. D
3. D	13. B
4. B	14. A
5. C	15. C
6. D	16. D
7. A	17. B
8. B	18. D
9. A	19. A
10. C	20. C

DA-6

1. B	11. B
2. D	12. D
3. A	13. C
4. C	14. B
5. A	15. A
6. C	16. B
7. B	17. D
8. D	18. C
9. A	19. A
10. C	20. B

DA-7

1. A	11. A
2. D	12. C
3. B	13. B
4. B	14. A
5. C	15. D
6. D	16. B
7. A	17. C
8. C	18. A
9. B	19. C
10. D	20. D

DA-8

1. D	11. B
2. A	12. C
3. B	13. A
4. C	14. D
5. B	15. C
6. A	16. A
7. D	17. B
8. C	18. C
9. A	19. D
10. D	20. A

DA-9

1. B	11. D
2. D	12. C
3. A	13. A
4. B	14. B
5. C	15. D
6. A	16. C
7. D	17. A
8. C	18. D
9. B	19. B
10. A	20. C

DA-10

1. C	11. C
2. D	12. A
3. A	13. D
4. B	14. A
5. C	15. B
6. D	16. C
7. B	17. D
8. A	18. A
9. D	19. C
10. B	20. B

DA-11

1. A	11. B
2. B	12. C
3. C	13. D
4. D	14. A
5. B	15. B
6. C	16. D
7. A	17. C
8. D	18. A
9. C	19. B
10. A	20. D

DA-12

1. D	11. C
2. B	12. A
3. A	13. D
4. C	14. A
5. B	15. B
6. C	16. C
7. D	17. D
8. A	18. B
9. D	19. A
10. B	20. C

ANSWER KEY Spelling Recognition Tests

DA-13

1. B	11. C
2. A	12. B
3. D	13. D
4. C	14. A
5. C	15. C
6. B	16. B
7. A	17. D
8. D	18. A
9. B	19. C
10. A	20. B

DA-14

1. C	11. D
2. A	12. B
3. D	13. A
4. B	14. C
5. C	15. D
6. A	16. B
7. D	17. A
8. B	18. C
9. C	19. B
10. A	20. D

DA-15

1. A	11. C
2. D	12. B
3. B	13. A
4. C	14. D
5. D	15. C
6. B	16. B
7. A	17. A
8. C	18. C
9. A	19. B
10. D	20. D

DA-16

1. B	11. C
2. C	12. D
3. A	13. A
4. D	14. C
5. B	15. B
6. C	16. A
7. A	17. D
8. D	18. B
9. A	19. C
10. B	20. D

DA-17

1. D	11. A
2. B	12. D
3. C	13. A
4. A	14. B
5. B	15. C
6. D	16. A
7. C	17. D
8. A	18. B
9. C	19. C
10. B	20. D

DA-18

1. C	11. A
2. D	12. B
3. A	13. C
4. C	14. B
5. B	15. D
6. D	16. C
7. B	17. A
8. C	18. B
9. A	19. D
10. D	20. A

DA-19

1. D	11. B
2. B	12. C
3. A	13. A
4. C	14. D
5. D	15. A
6. B	16. C
7. A	17. B
8. C	18. D
9. D	19. B
10. A	20. C

DA-20

1. C	11. D
2. A	12. A
3. D	13. C
4. B	14. B
5. C	15. D
6. D	16. A
7. B	17. C
8. A	18. B
9. C	19. D
10. B	20. A